VISITIN CHURCH

A Journey Exploring Effective Digital

Christian Community

PETER DEHAAN

ISBNs:
    978-1-948082-61-7 (e-book)
    978-1-948082-62-4 (paperback)
    978-1-948082-63-1 (hardcover)

Library of Congress Control Number: 2021912833

Published by Rock Rooster Books, Grand Rapids, Michigan

Credits:
    Developmental editor: Kathryn Wilmotte
    Copy editor/proofreader: Robyn Mulder
    Cover design: Taryn Nergaard
    Author photo: Chelsie Jensen Photography

To Gabe Hartfield

Contents

Why Online Church?

We've just spent a year with much of the world subsisting in various degrees of lockdown, isolation, and social distancing. In response to this, many churches went online to serve their congregations remotely. We hope we're moving out of this phase to return to normal, or at least a new normal that's not so objectionable.

So why publish a book about virtual church experiences and recommendations when we don't expect to need it anymore?

First, though we hope to move forever past the need to attend church remotely, we may one day find ourselves back there. This may be due to a variant strain of the virus reasserting itself or an unknown threat emerging that forces history to repeat itself.

We hope this will never happen. But if this does occur, we should be ready to react fast and respond well.

Second, and more importantly, we must acknowledge that a subset of Christians cannot attend church in person. There are many reasons for this. This may be due to a lack of transportation or the absence of a church nearby. It may be for medical reasons, either to protect themselves from the germs of others or to protect others from a condition they carry.

Some people grapple with time conflicts—often work schedules or caregiver responsibilities—that keep them away while others meet. The aged and infirm may face challenges that make attending in person too challenging. Still others struggle with social anxieties that hinder their face-to-face participation.

In too many instances—even before the pandemic—these folks have gone forgotten and underserved. This has happened for too long. For them, and all those who will follow, we must persist in providing a quality and accessible online church experience.

Finally, some fear that we will never again gather in large groups for any sustained period. A worst-case scenario is that online church and online spiritual community will become our new normal. Today, we must prepare for that possibility. Though I pray we will never realize this future and think it's an unlikely development, we must acknowledge that it could occur. If it does, may the church of Jesus be ready.

That's why we need a book exploring the digital, virtual, online church.

Regardless of what the future holds, we turn it and our concerns over to Father God. May the lessons we've learned now about online church empower us to meet the needs of *all* of Jesus's followers going forward, no matter the situation.

This narrative focuses on the human aspect of online church to help us most ably meet people where they are and form a best practices paradigm. As we do so, we'll see online services falling into two categories: custom content produced for an online audience, and streaming or replicating an in-person service to watch over the internet. Both options have their strengths and weaknesses, along with diverging viewer expectations.

Though I'll cover some technology tools used for online church, due to the rapid changes of innovation, consider these resources as generic directions to pursue and not specific recommendations to implement.

Now, let's visit our first online church.

A Quick Pivot

Sunday, March 15, 2020

It's Sunday morning and time to go to church. But my wife and I don't head to our car. Instead, we make our way to our living room. We sit in front of the TV in expectation of watching church online. We wait with excitement, anticipating a fresh way of encountering God. But we also mourn that we'll not experience sweet community with our friends, fellow followers of Jesus.

This year began like most others, full of promise for a new beginning, a fresh start for the coming year. Brimming with expectation for the potential that 2020 held, people everywhere planned as they hoped for what the next twelve months would offer.

Yet soon after we turned the pages on our calendars to the month of January, we heard rumblings of a distant threat from a faraway land. As the days marched on, the rumblings grew louder, and the menace moved closer. Week by week, the enemy approached us in the United States, just as it encroached on every other country in the world. Information and misinformation abounded. Experts contradicted one another about the severity of this unseen enemy and the prescription to deal with this unprecedented virus. Colleges sent students home. Those sporting events that continued often did so without the presence of fans. Decision-makers everywhere wrestled over how to best respond to something that no one fully understood.

Our church leaders grappled with this too, desiring to determine the best response to keep our church community healthy and safe. Four days ago, they announced their decision: "We have decided to move our Sunday services to an online format for the next two Sundays (March 15 and March 22)."

So we spend Sunday at home. We'll watch church online this week and next, resuming services as normal by the end of March. This announcement carries a link to our church's Facebook page. Candy, my wife, fiddles with her smartphone, trying to connect the tiny image on social media to our television set, something we have never done but know is possible.

An unfamiliar interface thwarts what should be a simple task. After several minutes of frustration, we consider retreating to my office computer and huddling in front of the monitor. Or we could watch the event separately, each on our own phone. Instead, she perseveres, hoping to accomplish our goal of experiencing church from the comfort of our living room.

Of course, this is a recorded video and not a livestream, so we can watch it at any time we wish. I should be more patient. I'm not. Growing in frustration, I pursue a different solution.

At last, I find a link to the recording on Vimeo, which is easy to cast to our TV. Soon the image of two familiar faces appears on our television. Recorded in a church office, our worship leader, standing next to our senior pastor, welcomes us to a new way of doing church. The next couple of weeks will be online to keep the most vulnerable in our community safe.

Though we aren't meeting as a large group, our lead pastor encourages us to gather in our homes and experience community, albeit in a smaller context. This could be with our small group, extended family, neighbors, or friends. But for this week, it's just Candy and me.

Although changing the format of our Sunday service for a few weeks, the rest of the church staff will function as normal. He concludes his introduction by saying, "Stay tuned as we figure this out as we go."

The next segment is just with our senior pastor. He outlines the schedule for today: a short teaching, a worship set (with the playlist on Spotify—though I don't understand how we are to use it during the service) and questions for us to discuss. He gives some announcements and shows a short video about an upcoming event. He prays and is ready to begin his teaching.

Recorded at a different time, he reads from Matthew 8:23–27, when Jesus calms the storm and rebukes his disciples for being afraid. Our pastor closes his teaching on fear by praying for God's blessings as we go through life's storms, just like we're experiencing today. His message takes twelve minutes, much less than his typical thirty to forty-minute sermons.

The third segment is just our worship leader. With only an acoustic guitar and his voice, he leads us in two songs to worship God. As the sound of the second song fades, our lead pastor steps into the shot to wrap up the service.

Calling today an "experiment" about how we gather and engage online, he leaves us with three questions. Candy jots them down. The whole service takes twenty-two minutes.

I'm most impressed that in only a couple of days they pieced together a meaningful service for us to engage with, using the tools and resources available to them without having much time to research and plan. In seven days, we can expect to encounter the next iteration of online church. I'm excited to see what it will look like.

I turn off the TV, and Candy reads the first question. We discuss it at length and move to the second and then the third. We enjoy an engaging conversation, enhancing the service we just experienced.

The time spent to connect to the recording, watch it, and discuss the follow-up questions is just over an hour, about the same length as a normal church service, minus travel time.

We eat lunch with much to contemplate.

With in-person services, our pastor sometimes sends us home with one question, but Candy and I seldom discuss the subject. By the time we wrap up our interactions with others and drive home, the question has faded from our memories, and we don't think to check our notes for a reminder.

Though I always try to talk about the message after the service, too many times I forget, and sometimes my efforts fall flat. But occasionally an insightful interaction takes place. Having probing talking points to use facilitates meaningful discussion which, with online church, we can consider right away.

Takeaway: What if we left every Sunday service armed with a couple of talking points—and then remembered to discuss them? This would require the minister to form the questions and us to remember to use them.

Adding Layers

Sunday, March 22, 2020

Much has changed in the past seven days. This week we learn that online church will continue through April 5, lasting four weeks instead of the initial two. Instead of the church staff continuing to work as normal, that has changed too: "We will not be holding any public gatherings, our offices are closed, and all of [our church] staff are working from home," says the email.

Once again, we go to church in our living room. Once again, Candy struggles to project Facebook on our TV. I admire her tenacity since I'm nowhere near as patient with technology.

Once again, Vimeo offers a simple solution. I appreciate our church's use of Vimeo as opposed to YouTube. Though YouTube is the second-most-used search platform and would offer greater discoverability, I see Vimeo as the safer option and the wiser destination.

While starting the video, I spot something we never know in advance when attending in person: the length of the service, though we can expect it to last from an hour to an hour and fifteen minutes. This recording is thirty-one and a half minutes. So, I know just how long church will take—or at least I think I do.

Our pastor of care and discipleship opens our service with a welcome and update. It looks like he recorded this segment in his home, on his phone, while holding it in selfie mode. I don't even notice this the first time I watch, so he pulls it off well, with no hint of awkwardness.

Despite our physical isolation, he says, it's important to know that "we are not alone." He invites us to like and share the post on Facebook so others can learn about our online service and join us—so that they will not be alone. He prays for the service that's about to follow.

The next segment is our senior pastor. He's also in his home, but he's not holding his phone. A stationary video camera captures him speaking, leaving both his hands free as he talks. He previews what to expect. An interesting addition is his plan to "create space with our morning today to share some time and engagement to interact as families." I'm intrigued.

He encourages us to bring ourselves fully into what unfolds online and interact with the service. He reminds us that email is now our primary way of communication. Those not receiving email updates should contact the church to join the list. He also mentions a podcast he started of a daily reflection to help us process this journey we're on. These options will enable us to stay better connected.

Before he begins his message, he asks us to share something from the past week that brought us joy and another item that caused us fear. I pause the recording so Candy and I can process what happened and share with each other. It's a significant way to move us into connecting with God. We resume the recording, and our pastor prays for the service and our community as we gather online and worship.

After the "amen" to his prayer, we jump to another segment, recorded at a different time and in another room of his house. I like the variety, but before he teaches, he asks us to again pause the video and discuss, "What does church mean to you?" Candy and I have an insightful time sharing our thoughts about church. Then we resume the recording.

"If your answer was that church is a place where you go for one hour on Sunday," says our pastor, "then church is nonexistent for you. Instead, let's talk about how the church is to treat one another," he continues, noting that fifty-nine times the Bible instructs how we are to treat one another. He starts with "love one another."

As instructed, we pause the recording a third time to draw a map of our neighborhood and list the neighbors we know by name. We don't make our map, but we do list our nearest neighbors.

When we return to the recording, he reads from Luke 10:30–37 about Jesus's story of the good Samaritan. Love is not how we feel about what we do. We love through our actions. To apply this, he refers us to the map we made earlier about our neighbors. "What do you know about them? Who is in need? Who is God leading you to pray for? Commit to pray for them every day this week. How can you engage with them and love them in a safe way?"

He gives us the option of pausing the video a fourth time to discuss this. Or we can do this later as a family. After he wraps up with a closing prayer, he segues to the next segment of the service.

We move to our worship leader and his wife, who come to us from their living room. Starting with Scripture and discussing the application, they invite us to worship with them in whatever way we feel comfortable. Together they form a pleasant-sounding duo who lead us into a time of powerful worship with two extended choruses.

As the music of the final song fades, the video switches to a closing clip of our senior pastor. Regardless of what's happening in our world around us, we are all connected, he says. More than ever, we need to love one another.

He ends with a blessing: "May the grace of the Lord Jesus Christ, and the love of God, and the fellowship of the Holy Spirit be with you all" (2 Corinthians 13:14). Then he tacks on "in these times."

Again, we enjoyed another meaningful online church service. Though having us pause four times for discussion may have been a bit too many, the first two times were especially significant—at least for me.

Though I expected the service to last about half an hour, with our discussion we approached forty-five minutes. It was good.

At three churches we have visited in person, the pastor left time mid-service for group discussion. The last time was at Church #57 in *More Than 52 Churches*. Though each time I appreciated the opportunity to interact with others, the first time dragged on too long for me, while the other two didn't allow for enough time. With a recorded service, however, we can pause for exactly the right amount of time, taking as little or as much as needed. It also allows people to not pause the recording if having a discussion doesn't interest them.

Today's video was both longer and more involved than last week's. Artfully placing the four clips together produced a meaningful service, and I'm most appreciative. I don't know the amount of prep time and postproduction work that this required, nor do I know how it compares with the time needed to produce an in-person service, but I appreciate their efforts and applaud the results.

Takeaway: Though we can't have two-way interaction with the people who lead our service online, leaving space for us to connect with each other is a great alternative.

Replicating a Live Service

Sunday, March 29, 2020

We're now into our third week of not being able to attend church in person and instead watching online. What started as a temporary two-week effort at isolation to stop the spread of the coronavirus is emerging into a protracted endeavor. We do, however, feel a bit of flexibility at being able to have family come over to spend time with us. This is what we'll do for church this week, with our daughter and her family coming to our house so we can watch church together and then share a meal. (Our son and his wife have a newborn. Their pediatrician encouraged them to maintain a stricter separation for the sake of their young son.)

Yet half of our family is here, and we're excited. This is the first we've seen them in several weeks. Our grandchildren, ages six and four, arrive equipped with quiet activities to keep them engaged during the service. Today, we'll experience their church online, which is wrapping up a series about Esther.

The church uses the Subsplash platform for their services. It provides an easy-to-use tool, accessible from their website. Our son-in-law pulls up the service on his phone and casts it to our TV. A countdown timer tells us to expect the service to begin in a couple of minutes. We sit back to prepare ourselves to experience God through this online presentation, while our grandchildren get situated for their own related arts-and-crafts project.

The church has two locations. They rent their primary space from a Christian school, whereas they have their own building for their second location.

Because it's more accessible, they recorded today's service at that site.

The counter hits zero, and the worship leader for that location welcomes us to the service and moves us into worship. A team of three—guitar, keyboard, and vocalist—stand appropriately distanced from each other on the stage. As they play and sing, lyrics appear on the bottom of the screen.

The music ends, and we cut to a recording of one of their pastors. He gives announcements, addresses the newer elements of virtual church, and asks for donations to help those in need. People can give at their website or through the church's app. He prays for us and the rest of the service.

A video plays to introduce the sermon.

Another of their pastors appears on the now-empty stage to give the sermon. He teaches us from Esther chapters 9 and 10 to conclude the series. Key points of his message appear on the bottom of the screen. They don't display the Scripture passages; however, they encourage us to read along from our Bibles or follow in their app, so we shouldn't need to see the words on the screen.

After thirty-plus minutes, he concludes his message. As he prays, the worship team eases back to the stage. The pastor says "amen" and exits, carrying with him the music stand he used for a pulpit. The camera shot pulls back to show all three of the worship team as they play the closing song.

The last shot is of the pastor who first welcomed us. He encourages us to go out into the world and serve God where he has put us and to advance the gospel of love.

This one-hour-and-eleven-minute service, though pieced together in segments, represents the same flow and format as one of their in-person services. Professionally accomplished, it replicates what happens on site every Sunday, albeit with no chance to interact with others.

Takeaway: If your circumstances and facility allow it, the easiest—although not necessarily the best—way to produce an online service is to replicate what you normally do every Sunday. Viewers will be most open to receive this with minimal complaint, aside from not being able to see or talk to their friends.

Church in Your Home

Sunday, March 29, 2020

L ater in the day I check out our church's service. The opening shot is our senior pastor from his home. He welcomes us to another installment of online church. He hasn't shaven in several days—a look I'm not used to seeing from him on Sunday mornings. Yet it feels appropriate given the situation. It's a reminder that he's working from home and living in isolation, something we're all doing. The casualness of the setting and his appearance draw me in. It feels good.

The length of the video is just shy of 32 minutes. Though some may feel gypped at not getting a full hour-long service, I'm not. I know we will get exactly what we need packed in this half-hour custom production. The idea of "church in your home" comes up. This may be the first mention of the concept. I like it. Just as the early church met in homes, we're doing that today, albeit in an atypical way. We are "isolated, but not alone," he reminds us. Though we can't meet in person, we can use technology to connect online. Though we may feel alone, that's not the reality of our situation.

"If you're watching by yourself," he says, "pick up the phone and call someone to watch with you." He mentions using FaceTime, which is an Apple-only video service. I presume it will synchronize the screens on each device. I'm not sure how I can accomplish this on Vimeo, but it is an intriguing idea.

Regardless of the method, he encourages us to engage and take part, not spectate. To accomplish this, we should remove distractions. When the time comes, pray and sing along. "Even if it might feel silly. It will be good for your soul." He outlines the order of events for today's online church and passes things over to our associate pastor.

He gives announcements, also from his home. He talks about our online guestbook. This, I assume, is a recent development. When we met in person, visitors could go to our welcome center before or after the service. With this in-person approach no longer an option, it—like many other things—is now online. This is a smart innovation, yet I wonder how many people will visit a church online during a pandemic. He also talks about some new online resources, but reiterates that the church is not just offering tools but tangible support too. He prays and announces the third segment.

Next up is our worship leader and his wife, coming to us from their home. It's an inviting and comfortable environment, drawing us into a time of worship. She reads from Psalms, he prays, and they lead us in song, accompanied by guitar. I try to sing along but find it uncomfortable. They sing beautifully and I don't. I feel my meager attempts to sing distract from their pure and engaging worship.

Next up is our lead pastor. His opening shot is him in his basement. It's dimly lit, and he whispers. He uses the setting to relate childhood memories of his family's basement and their noisy furnace. It's a powerful object lesson. He asks us to pause the video and discuss two questions while he moves to a different location in his house. From the second room, he completes his message, expertly providing a profound teaching in about twelve minutes. He gives us a homework assignment and makes a handoff to the next segment of today's online service.

Our student ministries director appears with her daughter from their home. The two of them share a practical tip about how we can love one another, especially during this trying time. I like how the two of them work together to communicate their idea. It's so much more effective than having one person make this suggestion.

We wrap up with a shot of our senior pastor in his home. He offers encouragement and gives us a blessing from Ephesians 3:20–21.

Takeaway: Don't feel a need to replicate an in-person service online. Consider innovative ways to create a meaningful virtual experience for your online audience, who may desire a fresh approach.

Church Attendance

Question 1

To discover additional information to shape this book and add diverse perspectives to its narrative, I conducted an informal survey of interested parties to gain a better perspective of online church. This is not scientific research. Readers shouldn't use these statistical results to justify actions or predict trends. Instead, this is feedback from seventy-seven people who wanted to support me as I wrote this book and those who were willing to take a survey to share their perspectives about online church.

About half the responses came from people who receive my weekly newsletter. I also solicited feedback on my blog, an online group, and social media.

I estimated the 10-question survey would take about two minutes to complete. Instead, participants spent an average of five and a half minutes. This was because over half of them gave additional written feedback, something I didn't expect but delighted in receiving. Most who gave written feedback did so at every opportunity. Ninety-one percent of the participants completed the survey, a much higher rate than normal.

Here are the statistical results of the ten questions, followed by my brief analysis of responses. I end each question with selected comments, edited for length and clarity.

Question 1. Before the coronavirus pandemic, how often did you go to church?

Every week:	80.5%
Most of the time:	11.7%
About half the time:	0.0%
At least once a month:	0.0%
Less than once a month:	7.8%

The high number of respondents who go to church every week is much greater than formally conducted studies, which various recent surveys put at about 25 percent. This shows that people who completed my online church survey have a much higher propensity for regular church attendance.

Additional comments:

- Before the virus, I attended in person about once a month and online the other three Sundays.

- Depends on what you call "church." If you mean meeting with other Christians to share, pray, or have coffee, then I "go to church" a few times a week.

- I had been ill for five years and was just ready to return when the pandemic hit. So, prior to that, the answer was weekly.

- I must ask what you mean by church. I fellowship often with other believers but do not attend an institutional corporate gathering.

- I work on Sundays.

- If I miss a Sunday, I watch a service on TV.

- The body of Christ gathers to worship, pray, and hear God's Word preached. Church attendance is essential for the Christ follower.

Takeaway: Most churches focus their attention on the people who show up, especially every Sunday. Look for ways to better engage with infrequent attendees, be it in person or online. More importantly, seek innovative online opportunities to meet the needs of those who can't, or won't, attend in person.

Livestream

Sunday, April 5, 2020

A friend mentions a church several states away. I decide to visit them online. Their website gives two ways to watch their services. One is an archive of past messages, and the other offers three livestream options: their website, Facebook, and YouTube. I pick YouTube.

The one-hour-and-36-minute video starts with a series of informational slides, which display along with an audio track of piano and light percussion. It sounds synthesized. This goes on for a long time, making me wonder if the recording is just an hour and a half of slides. But after 25 minutes a countdown timer appears, along with some majestic nature scenes.

With about three minutes left on the timer, a host appears. He welcomes us to the service. "The church is not a building," he says. "It's the people." He offers encouragement, reads Scripture, and requests continued faithful giving. "It's a way to say thanks to God." He lists four ways to donate. For the remaining time on the counter, the outdoor scenes switch to videos of the church members interacting, worshiping, and serving.

The counter hits zero, and a "Welcome home" slide appears.

Their associate pastor gives his greeting in a pre-recorded message. Thirty minutes into the recording, we switch to worship. Although the worship team is on stage, the guitar player, who welcomes us, confirms that the sanctuary is empty, and that they are "worshiping an audience of one." He encourages everyone to worship freely by singing from their homes and offering physical displays of worship to God as they feel comfortable. "God inhabits the praises of his people," he says, paraphrasing Psalm 22:3.

There are eight on the worship team, all socially distanced and by a wide margin. Fortunately, the large stage easily accommodates them. Multiple cameras—both handheld and on a boom—give us an engaging array of shots. We sing several songs, lasting about 25 minutes. The professional presentation feels equal parts concert and worship.

We then cut to a shot, also recorded earlier, of their discipleship pastor. He mentions some of the personal needs their church addressed in recent weeks, asking for donations so they can continue this outreach. He wraps up, and a short video plays to introduce the sermon series.

This is their third week of doing online church. In what looks like the church lobby, the pastor sits on a stool behind a simple stand. He has an audience of three, all spaced at least ten feet apart, along with a couple of camera operators. He reads the Scripture passage for today from 1 Corinthians 10:6–13 and launches into his message. The key points from his sermon, along with Scripture, appear at the bottom of the screen.

As he concludes his message, he stands and moves away from his podium, taking a few steps forward. Until now, he has focused his attention on the three people present. Now he looks at the camera and talks directly to his online audience. He gives an invitation for people to follow Jesus and prays for all who are listening.

To conclude the service, a video from the kids' pastor plays. He thanks us for visiting and watching their virtual church experience. Though the community is not in person, it still exists online. He mentions online groups that they are setting up. He also asks for donations. And he encourages people who gave their hearts to the Lord to contact the church to let them know.

This is the third time they mention giving in the service. It seems a bit much—too much for many people, especially those looking in from the outside. Yet, to be fair, each mention of donations comes from a different person, which I suspect they recorded at distinct times. It's quite possible that none were aware of the repetition—or it could be they really need the money.

He wraps up by inviting people to return next Sunday.

* * *

Large churches with an established infrastructure and an assortment of technical tools at their disposal, along with the staff to run them, will find it much easier to produce an engaging virtual church encounter. This doesn't rule out smaller churches, however, who may lack in the areas of technology, resources, and expertise, from producing a compelling online church experience. Simple also works.

The key is to put forth your best effort and fine-tune it as you go.

Takeaway: Isolated people crave connection, even if it's remote. Your online church service may be a significant lifeline for them.

~

Maundy Thursday

Thursday, April 9, 2020

An email alerts us to an online Maundy Thursday service, also known as Holy Thursday, something our church has never done before. The opening shot is side-by-side feeds with our worship leader on the left and our senior pastor on the right. It's not a service as much, he says, as an experience.

Our worship leader reads from Mark 14:12–16, and then our pastor teaches about the passage. In what later becomes known as Communion, Jesus and his disciples celebrate the Passover Seder (meal) together. It occurs in a person's home, just as we gather in our homes today. The celebration is an annual remembrance of God delivering his people from captivity in Egypt. There was a plague that "passed over" God's people but afflicted each Egyptian household.

The next reading continues the story in Mark 14:17–21, read by our worship leader. It's about Jesus's prediction that one of them will betray him. Each one asks, "It's not me, is it?" suggesting that they each realize their own shortcomings. Our pastor reminds us that today we continue to live in a sin-filled world, where any of us could cave in and betray Jesus. But he can redeem us and save us from our mistakes.

The third segment covers the Communion observance. The video switches to a shot of just our pastor. Because of our home-bound isolation, we're not able to celebrate this significant ritual together. As a concession, our pastor sends us to our kitchens to find what we have available that can substitute for the bread and the wine. He reads from Mark 14:22–25, interspersing the reading with him eating his sourdough bread and then drinking his apple juice—his substitutions, based on what he had available.

Then he prays.

But this isn't the end of the story. There's one more verse, Mark 14:26, where they sing a hymn before leaving. The shot switches back to our worship leader, who leads us in singing "How Great Thou Art," with guitar accompaniment.

He concludes by encouraging us to use this experience to reflect on what Jesus has done for us.

Fade to black.

The experience lasts less than twenty minutes, reminding us that significance doesn't depend on length but on substance.

Takeaway: To best engage people online, seek fresh approaches to reframe what you've always done—or have never done—to connect with them in meaningful ways.

Easter Sunday

Sunday, April 12, 2020

It's Easter, Resurrection Sunday. Though we won't celebrate our risen Savior in person, we will celebrate together online. At four weeks into our ordeal, I'm weary and lonely, frustrated that our state's two weeks of isolation turned into four and then more. When will we get a reprieve? Yet, this doesn't dampen my expectation for today and all the significance that it carries. We turn on our TV and connect to our church's online programming for this special day.

The service opens with a professionally produced video that in two and a half minutes succinctly tells us who Jesus is and what he did for us. It's a fitting introduction for our time together.

After a poignant moment of silence and a darkened screen, we segue to the next part. A church attendee reads the resurrection story from his printed Bible, while his son reads along on his device. Following this opening passage, the shot switches to another person reading the text and another and another. In rapid succession, they collectively read from Matthew 28:1–7, with each reader's section edited together to produce a dramatic impact. They conclude with "He is risen from the dead."

Aside from the impact of the passage, it's comforting to see friends and familiar faces reading today's text. Though this reminds me of how long it's been since I've last seen them, it also cheers me to glimpse them again, albeit from a distance.

The third scene is our senior pastor welcoming us from his house. I think it's the same place he sat for our Maundy Thursday service, just three days ago. He acknowledges the awkwardness of us meeting online and not in person. But despite our physical separation, he invites us to celebrate together.

Our associate pastor follows, also from his home. He gives announcements and reminds us that today is the last day to sign up to be in a virtual community. He also recaps how we can stay connected online.

Next, we're treated to another montage of the people from our church family saying hi, how much they miss us, or how excited they are for when we can meet in person again. Seeing their smiling faces and compelling waves warms my heart.

Our pastor opens his message talking about disruption, which is an emotion we can all identify with through our various circumstances and experiences over the past few months. He asks us to pause the video to discuss or journal some of the key things in our life that seem out of sorts, forming our messy place.

After we share our thoughts with our extended family, he reads the Easter story from John 20:1–10 as we move from our messy place into something more hopeful. "There is resurrection that comes out of death." With us subsisting in quarantine, he says, much of our life reminds us of death, of things we've lost or cannot experience, but "amid all this God still promises us life."

Our pastor then reads another resurrection account from Luke 24:1–8. "Why are you looking for the living among the dead?" he asks, smartly summarizing the key point of the passage. That's our hope for the day, our encouragement. Look for resurrection around us and not what we've lost. "God gives us new life."

He prays and we move into the closing set. Our worship leader and his family introduce the segment. The final song, "O Praise the Name," comes from nine locations, shown on our screen in a three-by-three grid. The song starts with musicians in four of the boxes and incrementally adds vocalists to fill in all nine. It's a creative approach with a powerful impact, both spiritually and emotionally. They wrap up by singing the chorus a cappella.

Our pastor concludes with an encouragement for us to take the resurrected hope of Jesus with us as we move into the days and weeks ahead. He gives us a blessing and the service ends. "Amen."

The video, clocking in at just under thirty minutes, is another reminder that we can enjoy a profound experience in a short amount of time. Our church expertly packed in meaningful content to produce a powerful service.

Takeaway: Producing online content allows for options that aren't available for in-person gatherings, and this special Easter service proves what a delight that creativity can be.

Online Participation

Question 2

After establishing a baseline of respondents' pre-pandemic church attendance habits, I asked about their online participation.

Question 2. When your church was online, how often did you watch?

Every week:	45.5%
Most of the time:	27.3%
About half of the time:	3.9%
At least once a month:	5.2%
Less than once a month:	18.2%

Compared to their in-person church attendance practices, online church engagement decreased a lot. Given the uncertainty of the situation, this is not a surprise.

Additional comments:

- Almost daily now.

- I also watch four to five other TV services on Sunday.

- I just can't find it helpful or interesting.

- I listened and watched once and did not care for it. There was no music, just suggested songs so you could listen to them on YouTube. The content of the sermon was superficial.

- I meet with friends outside, mask on, around a firepit.

- I watch various services on TV every week.

- We went online, and I couldn't take it for long. Being single, the isolation is much worse.

- My church doesn't have too much of an on-line presence.

- I started off watching faithfully, but I found the experience unsatisfying.

- We have always attended [in person] and watched other pastors online throughout the week.

- We listened to different churches and pastors during the lockdown.

Takeaway: According to this survey, many people failed to transition from in-person church to online. Look for ways to make your online viewing options more attractive to them. This will allow you to better address people who will continue to pursue online opportunities, as well as better position your church in the event of a future need to return online.

Virtual Community

Friday, April 17, 2020

Our church has three opportunities for people to connect outside of the Sunday morning service. One is service teams, where people work together as a group to perform a function for the church or a service to the community. Service teams provide the opportunity for people to connect with each other as they work together to accomplish a common goal.

A second connection opportunity is small groups. These gatherings of ten or so people meet every other week, usually on Sunday evenings. It's a time to hang out, get to know each other better, and share life. In between scheduled meetings, the group supports its members as they encounter the difficulties of life. It's a key source of encouragement and Christian community.

A third connection option is Breaking Bread. This is a low-commitment opportunity to meet other people. The premise is that three families or individuals commit to get together three times around a shared meal, snack, or coffee.

Most service groups halted when the church went online. And though the small groups continued to meet for a time, they too paused or continued at a distance, using videoconference, email, and text messages to stay in touch. Breaking Bread also stopped. My wife and I had just completed the first of three meetings with our new group, when the majority decided to not meet the second and third time because of health concerns.

To fill the void, the church introduced Virtual Community. This functions like a small group over Zoom. To facilitate group formation, all interested people filled out an online form. Instead of asking when people *wanted* to meet and complicating the task of forming groups, the form instead asked when we were *not* available. The group for Candy and I met Friday evenings, since no one said they were unavailable that day. During our first meeting, however, we discovered no one in the group wanted to meet on Fridays; it was inconvenient for us all. We switched to Thursdays.

The group gathered online every other week. Our leader aptly managed our meetings, helping us to connect and engage with each other. We welcomed the time together since most people in the group had minimal or no interaction with others outside their homes.

As we moved into summer, however, some work opportunities, outdoor activities, and social events reemerged—albeit not at church. It became harder for members to make our meetings. Our numbers dwindled, and we eventually stopped. I enjoyed the time together and the connections we were making. I wish our group had lasted longer.

Takeaway: Providing connection opportunities is essential for support and encouragement, especially when mandated isolation makes gathering in person impossible. Yet to realize the best results from this opportunity, everyone must commit to make it a priority.

~⁓~

Engaging and Effective

Sunday, April 19, 2020

I receive a tip to check out a church that's about 30 miles away. Though in normal times I could go there in person, now my only option is online. The service begins with opening slides that display for a couple of minutes. I'm excited about what I'll experience. My church is medium-sized, and two weeks ago I shared a larger church's livestream. Today's virtual destination is a smaller, rural church.

A young pastor and his wife give a welcome and banter a bit as they drink coffee and hold up their mugs for all to see. She extends her arm to take a selfie of them and their cups. She'll post it online and will ask everyone to post theirs. Then they'll vote on the best one. It should be a fun time of interaction.

This spontaneous intro is most engaging. Their playfulness draws me in. I forget I'm watching church online because it feels like we're sitting across the kitchen table from each other having a cozy conversation. Even though we're separated by time and distance, I feel connected.

The video ends, and the screen goes black. The opening slide reappears for a couple more minutes.

The next segment cuts to another home with two women (I presume mother and daughter). Mom reads Scripture (Psalm 146), and they sing as Mom plays the keyboard. It's simple and worshipful. After a couple of songs, they wrap up with "thanks for worshiping with us."

The third segment comes from another portion of the pastor's home. His wife gives some updates. Then she announces the offering, stressing that it's only for those able to give. She encourages giving in faith, trusting God with their finances. What she doesn't say is how they will receive the donations. I assume members know what to do. Then she prays for the service and those watching online. Her prayer flows forth with passion and sincerity, drawing me into God's presence. With the "amen," a slide pops up. Although there's the same musical interlude, the wording on the image is different, showing two options for how people can give.

The fourth segment is in the same setting as the third, although this time we see only their pastor. "Thank you for tuning in to another rendition of online church," he says to welcome us, regardless of what state we are in, be it geographic or emotional.

Today he starts a new series from the book of Philippians. Instead of opening with Philippians 1:1, however, he begins with the backstory to the church of Philippi as found in Acts 16. He closes with prayer and wraps up with an invitation for those in need to contact him.

The background music returns, this time with a third slide that says, "See you next week."

The service had a comfortable feel to it. It was informal and effective, conversational throughout. I felt connected and received encouragement.

Takeaway: You don't need a lot of technology to produce an engaging online service, just the desire to connect with people. The key is to be yourself.

* * *

Much later, I email the church. Pastor Keith and I have a meaningful exchange. He shares that they had just moved to the area and started working at the church when the pandemic hit. His first decision as their pastor was to discontinue their in-person Sunday services. He did some quick learning to put together their virtual service. After he produced an online church experience for a couple of months, they moved to streaming the services, with some people attending in person and others watching online.

He shares a profound insight that stays with me. "Streaming is the new front door to church attendance. I don't think people will come in the door who haven't seen us online first."

Takeaway: We should treat our online services as an outreach opportunity to connect with visitors and spiritual seekers, producing an engaging service to draw them into our faith community, whether it's online or in person.

Powerful and Professional

Sunday, April 26, 2020

Today's virtual destination is another faraway church. They had an online experience on YouTube prior to the pandemic, making them well prepared to meet the needs of remote worshipers when it became necessary to do so. Besides a special online service, they also post the sermon in a separate video. Both are available through their website and on YouTube.

Their online service opens with a series of informational slides, background music, and a countdown timer. I have five minutes to wait. But before the counter hits zero, two people appear, a man and a woman, in a socially distanced setting. They give some announcements, interspersed with playful banter. I'm excited about what will come next.

The timer reaches zero, and worship begins. The team leads from the stage. Though it looks live, I don't see any hint of worshipers and assume they recorded it in an empty auditorium for the online service. A few minutes in, a collage pops up with feeds of over a dozen members singing along with gusto from the safety of their homes. The individual feeds change rapidly to reveal many more who sing along in corporate worship, albeit socially distanced from their homes. Suddenly it no longer feels as awkward for me to join in and sing from the comfort of my house.

After several minutes, the music winds down. One of the guitar players reads Scripture and prays. I expect the sermon to follow, but I'm wrong. There's more worshiping through song. When they finish their second set, a smartly produced video plays that leads into the sermon by their senior pastor.

He opens with a "family meeting" to discuss the difficulty of not gathering in person and the care they are taking in deciding when it will be safe—and wise—to do so again. Despite that, the focus should not be on how soon they can meet again in person, but on how to best fulfill their mission to function as a church in the meantime. Regardless of what their Sunday meetings look like, the church is still the church. He then shares some stories of the church in action despite these unusual circumstances.

Eventually he moves into the message about the life of Job and the hardships he endured, seeing God more clearly than ever. He wraps up his message and prays.

Communion follows. A chat message says, "If you regularly attend one of our campuses, head to your campus's Facebook page for a time with Communion meditation. If you don't attend a campus, stick with us right here." The worship team plays and then sings. Though they give no direction, I assume we are to engage in an individual self-guided Communion experience. Although I desire to reflect on Jesus's great gift to us, I don't search for something to drink and eat. I'm not sure if I lack the motivation to do so or feel I can have the desired spiritual impact without the need for these physical reminders.

The Communion time lasts about five minutes, but I remain mired in the role of observer and don't mentally participate as I had hoped. This marks a failure on my part, but I'm not sure if having the physical elements would have changed the outcome.

To conclude the service, one of the worship leaders encourages members to go to their campus Facebook page for a Facebook Live session to connect with their community.

But the online service isn't over. Another pastor gives a wrap-up and prays. A series of slides—I suspect the same ones that appeared before the service—display for the next ten minutes as background music plays. One slide encourages people needing prayer to email the church.

Throughout the service, a chat feed scrolls to the right of the video. There's much interaction, not only from a church staffer but also from viewers who chat with each other, ask questions, and offer encouragement. Even during the closing slides, the chat continues, although not as active as earlier. One message from the church staffer gives the address of where to mail contributions.

The video ends, and the final chat message is from a viewer who writes, "Thank you so much! What a powerful service this morning!"

I agree.

Takeaway: What can you do with your online church experience to help people interact and connect with each other?

Drive-in Church

Sunday, May 3, 2020

After a couple of months of virtual church services, one church announced a switch to Drive-in Church starting Sunday, May 3. I can't attend in person, but I do hope to experience it online. The service will start at 11, but the people should arrive at 10:30 to find a parking space and to participate in some pre-church activities for the kids.

Though they don't share a video of the service, they do post pictures. Cars, parked in every other space, fill the lot. Many people bring chairs, which they set in front of their vehicles. Others back into their space and pop the hatchback to view the service.

The rest, it appears, listen from the front seats of their cars.

They'll do Drive-in Church every Sunday until they feel it's safe to return to in-person meetings.

Disappointed at not being able to experience Drive-in Church online, I explore their website, looking for something else to watch. The church had been streaming their services on Facebook prior to the pandemic. When they had to pause their in-person services, they produced a special online version, including one for Easter. Here's what happened on Resurrection Sunday:

The caption above the Facebook video proclaims "Join us for our online Easter service. No virus will stop us from celebrating this historic day." I click the play button.

Though they don't provide the source, the online service opens with a professional video of people happily sharing exciting news with one another, reminiscent of the good news 2,000 years ago that Jesus rose from the dead. After a dramatic fade to black, the next scene, from their church facility, is of the worship and youth director who welcomes us to their Easter service. He reads from Matthew 28:8–9, which ends with, "They came to him, clasped his feet and worshiped him." This is their goal today, to worship him.

Cut to the next scene of the worship team of five, each playing or singing "Glorious Day" from their respective homes.

The fourth shot is back to their church building, but this time with their lead pastor. He thanks the people for joining them in this "unique way" for Easter. Though their method of gathering is different, their intent of why they celebrate stays the same.

He preaches his prerecorded message to the camera guy (who I suspect is also the worship director) in an otherwise empty sanctuary. He encourages people who are watching to snap a picture of themselves to post online, whether dressed in their Sunday best or still in their pajamas. After his 20-minute message about the resurrection of Jesus, he closes in prayer.

The next segment is back to their worship team, and they play another song, again recorded from their respective homes. We then return to the pastor who closes the service with a Communion reading from 1 Corinthians 11. He encourages people to find some juice and some bread or crackers in their homes as they contemplate what Jesus did when he died for them. They celebrate Communion as a church community, despite being in scattered locations.

After Communion, he thanks people for their generous giving and asks for their continued support. People can mail their donation to the church, give online, or use the Give app. He ends with an update on when they may again meet in person. The decision will be made on a week-to-week basis.

Takeaway: Being adaptable and open to adjust is the best way to react to changes, especially when they seem to occur daily. This includes creating custom content, streaming a simulated service, or having Drive-in Church.

Mother's Day

Sunday, May 10, 2020

I wish my mother happy Mother's Day early in the morning by email and later in the day by phone. Our children do the same for their mom. I contemplate the critical but too-often-underappreciated role that moms play in the lives and development of their children. I expect that part of today's online service at our home church will address this theme.

I guess correctly. The online service opens with several dozen clips of kids saying what they like about their mothers and wishing her happy Mother's Day. The youngest children barely get out "I love you, Mom." With many, I struggle to understand what they say, but I'm sure their moms know. Other children, a bit older, try to say more. And they do, with varying degrees of success. The teens share their appreciation too, not out of obligation but from the overflow of their hearts.

Collectively they preach a poignant Mother's Day sermon. This could be enough, but there's more.

Our ministry director welcomes us. She also says, "Happy Mother's Day," reads from Colossians 3:12–17, and prays for our service, inviting God to enter our hearts as we hear the message and worship him.

Ever creative in how he introduces his message, our senior pastor opens with a clip of him in his workout room, strolling on his treadmill. He talks about being sad. Despite our efforts to look at the positive during our crisis and seek to be happy, "it's okay to be sad." He asks us to name something that has made us down. We can stop the recording to talk, journal, or draw a picture of what makes us sad. As we do, he's going to take a shower and change. Then he'll continue today's message.

The next shot of him comes from a different place in his house, a room where we've been hanging out on recent Sundays. He continues with his sermon series, talking about the Israelites in the desert. It's their in-between space. It's not where they've been, and it's not where they're going. Instead, it's where they've been stuck for forty years. What can they do with this space they're in? What should we do with the space *we're* in?

He reads from Exodus 17:1–6, where Moses strikes the rock and God causes water to gush forth for his thirsty people. Our minister points out three things. First, the people aren't wrong to be upset about being in the desert. Second, the problem begins with what they do about their feelings: they complain and blame Moses. Last, Moses responds differently. He takes his pain to God and honestly shares his heart.

We can do what Moses did. Or what David did when he laments to God in Psalm 13. Another passage, Psalm 91:14–16, shows us God's response when we seek him amid difficulty. This is our lesson from the desert.

In response, we sing songs to God, led by our worship leader and his wife from their home. Our minister reminds us of Philippians 4:6–7, about not being anxious about anything but bringing our concerns to God in prayer. Our students' director wraps up the service by encouraging us to connect online and reminding us of our church's podcast.

Today's service smartly balanced our celebration of moms, while not abandoning our current sermon series either, giving a message for everyone that was both timely and encouraging.

Takeaway: For holiday Sundays, whether in person or online, seek balance between the day's theme and an experience everyone will find meaningful.

Reasons for Attending Church

Questions 3 and 4

The next two questions on my survey explored church attendees' motivations for going. First, I asked for *all* the reasons they went. Then I asked for their *primary* purpose.

Question 3. Why do you go to church? (check all that apply)

To worship God:	92.2%
To spend time with other Christians:	81.8%
To hear an inspiring message:	61.0%
I feel I should:	24.7%

Out of habit:	19.5%
For the sake of a family member or friend:	18.2%
I feel guilty if I don't:	13.0%

People who completed the survey had a wide-ranging array of reasons for attending church. The opportunity to worship God ranked highest, followed closely by the opportunity to spend time with other believers. Trailing these two primary reasons, in third place, was to hear an inspiring message, with only two-thirds of people attending church for that reason.

From this pool of church attendees, it's sobering that they see the sermon as their third most important reason for attending. And this comes from a group of people with a higher-than-normal propensity for church attendance.

Another interesting observation is that this group of people place a much higher emphasis on community than on sermon, yet many church services do little to provide the opportunity for interpersonal connection.

Additional comments:

- Also, to grow spiritually.

- Because I belong to Christ's body.

- Draw nearer to God and he will draw nearer to you [from James 4:8.] When I know more about him, I can try to process how very much he cares for and loves me.

- I do not think "inspiring message" is the right term. When I hear a message, I think more in terms of God's word through his messenger.

- I include "out of habit" as it's a good practice to keep even on Sundays when I don't feel like going. It's more of a spiritual discipline. Also,

I know it's good for me, as well as good for me to worship God corporately.

- I worship God more outside of a formal church service. It is possible to worship God with your life.

- To be fed.

- To learn, grow, worship, praise, congregate, build relationships, and serve others.

- To worship with the body of Christ in unity and grow.

Question 4. What is the *primary* reason you go to church? (check one)

To worship God:	64.9%
To spend time with other Christians:	18.2%
To hear an inspiring message:	7.8%
Out of habit:	2.6%
I feel I should:	2.6%

I feel guilty if I don't: 2.6%

For the sake of a family member
or friend: 1.3%

Within this online survey group, it was clear that their primary reason for going to church is to worship God. Though the opportunity to spend time with other believers followed in a distant second, many of their comments reflected a profound loss in not being able to enjoy personal interaction with other believers. (The next question will confirm this numerically.)

Less than 8 percent of this group listed the sermon as their major reason for going to church. Yet several of the respondents' churches only post their sermons online.

Additional comments:

- "Church" is meeting with other Christians.

- For the feeling, the passing of the peace, the hugs and kisses, the feeling of being up close and personal with everyone involved.

- I like to sing in the choir and hear and feel voices and the intake of breath of the other singers. Online only allows for some of this.

- I miss being with other Christians, but I have several Christian friends I speak with on the phone to fill the gap.

- It drives me nuts when Christians mention going to "church" to worship God. Aren't we to do that all the time each day?

- Partly as an example to my kids. We are in a difficult church situation.

- Also, to minister and serve others.

- Sometimes I don't feel like going to church, but I'm always glad once I get there. God will use a song, the message, Scripture, or an interaction with someone to encourage me or help me grow.

- To worship God corporately. You can worship God anywhere.

Takeaway: Though the responses from this survey are not likely to mirror the views of your church's attendees, ask them why they go to church and which reason is the most important to them. Then respond as appropriate.

ASL and Other Online Options

Sunday, May 24, 2020

A friend recommends a church to check out. Their website has many options for online services. A banner on their homepage highlights the "Watch Live" option, which takes me to a page of livestream videos, with three times on Sundays: 10:15 a.m., 11:30 a.m., and 3:00 p.m. They also have other programs for online viewing, including women's ministry, Wednesday evening service, and the kids' program. A countdown timer tells me how long before the next live service begins, ticking off the seconds. They also have a YouTube page with many videos.

Their website menu also has a "Watch" option, with three sections. One is for sermons. The second one repeats the "Watch Live" option. The third is for translations. (Linguistic purists may assert that translation deciphers the written words of one language for another, while interpretation does so for the spoken word. In our context, however, we'll use these words interchangeably, as most people do.)

"Translations" intrigues me and gives me three possibilities: Spanish, Chinese, and ASL (American Sign Language). I check them all out.

The Spanish and Chinese options play a video of the main service, with English subtitles and dubbed audio in Spanish or Chinese—at least that's my assumption, since I know neither tongue. The English audio plays softly during the worship set. The interpreter doesn't sing but speaks. I assume he says the song's lyrics. During the message, the minister's audio is muted with the interpreter speaking. Interestingly, the slides before and after the service are in English.

The ASL service interests me the most because this came up as an unmet need in my research. One of my survey respondents mentioned this in his comments. His frustration in this area enabled me to comprehend the complexity of serving the deaf community and to discard my simplistic solutions and uninformed perspectives.

The video of the ASL service opens with a shot of the side of the stage, centering on a stool, which I presume is for the ASL interpreter. The upper right-hand corner of the screen displays information slides. Background music plays. This wouldn't matter to a person who can't hear, but it would be a pleasant feature for their hearing-enabled companions. Occasionally a person walks into or through the shot, either unaware of or not concerned about the video feed. This continues for fifteen minutes as we wait for the service to start.

The service begins with an introduction from one of their pastors. His image appears in the box in the upper right-hand corner. An interpreter moves into the main shot and sits on the stool. Though she missed his first few sentences, she jumps in and signs what he says. Though I don't know ASL, I comprehend some of her signs.

Next, we move into the worship set. Our interpreter remains the focus of the shot with the worship team in the upper right-hand corner of the screen. The words of the song display in the section beneath a shot of the worship team. The ASL interpreter has a pleasant countenance, which is both inviting and worshipful. She draws me in. The worship set ends with prayer. We move to a shot of the pastor who opened the service. He prays and introduces the offering, which people can now give online.

They cut to a scene of the stage for the sermon. As the pastor speaks, our interpreter scurries away and another one moves into view and begins signing. It's a quick, smooth transition. Our first interpreter signed for about twenty-five minutes, and I had wondered how long she'd be able to continue. For her sake, I'm glad she has a break.

The pastor introduces a video, which also displays in the upper right-hand corner. Our interpreter continues her work for this video. After about 30 minutes, midway through the sermon, the second interpreter leaves and the first one returns.

The minister continues his sermon about the church in Laodicea from Revelation 3:14–22 and after a while our interpreters switch again.

The minister says he's about out of time. The interpreter points to the watch on her wrist. I'm not sure if this is part of ASL or a signal to the other interpreter, but they switch again. We're now back to the first interpreter who leads us through the rest of the service. This includes the pastor's conclusion to his message and the final number.

With the "amen" to the worship leader's prayer, our interpreter exits the shot. Slides—the same ones we saw at the beginning—play in the upper right-hand corner of the screen for a few more minutes, and the video ends.

The recording lasted over two hours. The first interpreter had three shifts, and the second one had two. Together they produced a most effective presentation of the service—at least in my opinion.

Out of curiosity, I later check out another one of their services. In it, three interpreters share signing duties. This is a powerful video service to a significant and underserved population. I applaud the church for providing it.

What most impresses me is that this church makes signing a priority in this livestream option. They keep the interpreter in the main part of the shot, making it easy for hearing-impaired people to see her every movement. This provides the maximum opportunity for deaf viewers to experience the service.

This is unlike other churches that include an ASL interpreter in their livestream. Every other time I've encountered this, the minister or worship team has been the focus of their shot, with the interpreter shown in the lower left-hand corner. This makes it harder for ASL viewers to catch what the interpreter signs. This is especially true on smaller displays.

* * *

American Sign Language (ASL) isn't a universal language. It's used in the United States and parts of Canada, but not so much in the rest of the world. This doesn't, however, imply that ASL uses English as its base. It doesn't.

ASL originated independently of English-language influence and is more closely affiliated with French sign language. In fact, it's a separate language, developed organically over time by deaf people, evolving just like oral communication. ASL, like spoken languages, has a unique grammar, syntax, and vocabulary, independent of English. It also has its own cultural context. It isn't simply English expressed through gestures.

In viewing ASL as a separate language, we can comprehend that many deaf people are bilingual, using both ASL and English. Just as other bilingual people may struggle to communicate in their second language, some deaf people prefer ASL and struggle with English, which is effectively their second language.

It's important we reorient our perception of deaf people to stop thinking of them only as a disabled group. Instead, we should broaden our understanding to view them as a language minority. In this way, we can use this critical distinction to reshape our view of how to best embrace the deaf community.

Providing closed captioning is a workable solution for some deaf people, but this is not true in all cases. Some ASL-speaking people don't know English. For others, their English proficiency—because it's their secondary language—doesn't allow them to comprehend the nuances of fast-moving English text.

To confirm the importance of ASL for the deaf community, an ASL Bible is now available to serve this underserved demographic. (See the reference section at the end of this chapter to learn more.)

According to Acutrans, a translation and interpretation provider, about "a million people in the United States use ASL as their primary language." Some claim that ASL is the third most used language in the United States, and others say it's the third most studied one, behind Spanish and French.

The Survey of Income and Program Participation (SIPP) from the United States Census Bureau shows there are close to one million people in the US who are functionally deaf. The Institute of Medical Sciences, however, puts the number higher, at 1.35 million or 0.57 percent of the population.

Globally, the World Health Organization estimates that 466 million people in the world have disabling hearing loss (6.1 percent).

Takeaway: What can your church do to better serve the deaf community and other language minorities?

(Relevant resources: deafbiblesociety.com, deaf.bible, deafchurchwhere.com, and deafmissions.com. Also see lifeprint.com/asl101/topics/history8.htm, nidcd.nih.gov/health/american-sign-language, and nad.org/resources/american-sign-language/what-is-american-sign-language.)

Variation and Innovation

Sundays, April 19–May 31, 2020

As we move through spring and approach summer, our produced online services continue to change, providing new iterations to fine-tune and enhance each week's production. We also receive periodic weekly updates, which are equally creative. Here are some of the variations and innovations we encountered.

An opening slide gives instruction: "How to get the most out of online church: Be fully present. Like, share, and comment. Worship, don't just watch." It's a smart reminder—which we see repeated—not to be passive observers of our online church, but to engage with the service (April 19).

A mid-week status update includes a testimony. Though a video recording of a person sharing their story can occur during an in-person service, it fits equally well—if not better—online, either in a service or apart from it. Again, seeing a familiar face helps me connect with my community and encourages me amid physical isolation (April 24).

The conclusions of many services provide connection options. These include listening to the church's new podcast, joining an email group (the first I remember hearing this option), and taking part in a virtual community. These serve as reminders that we don't need to navigate this unprecedented time of physical isolation in emotional separation. We can—and we should—journey with others in the best way possible (April 26).

Though we've usually experienced our worship time from the intimate setting of someone's house, today two pairs of people split this time, with each duo leading us in song from their respective homes. I like the variety and the opportunity to see more people take part in the online service (May 3).

The opening greeting comes, not from a staff member, but from attendees. Three videos play in succession to open the service. Each one features a family who provides their own spin on giving an inviting welcome. I enjoy seeing their fresh faces. It's an engaging start to the service (May 17 and May 24).

A Saturday update is a long-form conversation between our pastor and one of our members. They discuss a plan to move forward, noting that flexibility is key because no one knows which direction the future may take. Our pastor ends with a simple, three-point instruction that is most appropriate given the frustration many people feel over the situation we're in. He says to be nice, be patient, and be engaged (May 30).

Though we've heard it before, it's worth repeating. We shouldn't watch the worship team lead us in song.

We should sing along with them, even if it feels awkward (May 31).

Takeaway: A simple approach for producing online content is to develop a format and plug segments into a template. Making weekly changes, however, to enhance the virtual experience results in a more engaging service. Don't we want that? Doesn't God deserve that?

First Midweek Outdoor Worship

Wednesday, June 17, 2020

As our days of mandated isolation turn into weeks and then months, the emotional toll of forced seclusion becomes a burden increasingly harder to bear. With rare exceptions, I have seen no one except immediate family for four months, and even those interactions involved restrictions.

Summer has opened the opportunity for outdoor activities—within limits—but I still feel alone and lonely. Though the lockdown accomplished what it intended and was wise to address for my physical health, the casualty has been my mental wellbeing. Many share this deep loss with me. Looking at my life holistically, I'm in worse shape now than when this ordeal first started.

So, when our church announces a midweek outdoor service, I'm thrilled. Though staff—both paid personnel and volunteers—will wear masks, face coverings are optional for everyone else since we'll be outside. The only expectation is to maintain social distancing, which seems a wise precaution.

Since there will be no projection system, our church emails us a link to the song lyrics. Candy and I download the pdf to our phones in preparation for the service.

We arrive early. This is in part because we're excited for an outing—any outing—and in part for an opportunity to interact with friends before the service. We've not seen these people for four months. This reunion arises as a significant social *and* spiritual relief from the tedium of our government-mandated seclusion.

As announced, the staff and volunteers wear masks, though few of the attendees do. Mostly we maintain social distancing, though some people can't suppress the occasional urge for a hug or handshake.

The service itself follows a typical Sunday format with announcements, music, and message. There's nothing noteworthy about what they say or do, except that we have experienced nothing like this in person for months. And the rural outdoor location, on a sunny evening, is a pleasant bonus. But these are not the reasons Candy and I are here.

Yes, we want to show our physical support of our church's first attempt at a public gathering since they paused their Sunday services in mid-March. Today our interest is more social than spiritual, although our social interactions will provide a much-needed spiritual connection with others. Today—and a similar outing next week—will serve as preparation, a prelude to holding outdoor meetings after the Fourth of July holiday weekend.

Today we encountered our first in-person church community in four months. Though I will soon forget the songs we sang and the message we heard, I won't forget the buzz of excitement over reconnecting with other like-minded followers of Jesus.

I can't wait to repeat the experience next week and then resume it in July.

Takeaway: Whether online or in person, look for fresh ways to connect isolated people and fill their emotional emptiness with meaningful interaction.

Second Midweek Outdoor Worship

Wednesday, June 24, 2020

This week we gather outdoors at a county park, only a few miles from where we used to hold our Sunday services. Though I didn't count the number of people last week, today it feels like more people have gathered. We strategically set up our lawn chairs around the park's picturesque stage, which often serves as a setting for photo shoots and a platform for weddings. Today the space hosts a church service.

As with last week, staff wear their face masks, but few others do. It's an idyllic summer evening, and we're glad to be together once again. Though our church's services always veer toward the informal, the outdoor setting makes our time together even more endearing. Like last week, there's a welcome and announcements, music, and message. It's like a low-key church service, albeit midweek. Though we've been experiencing these things online for four months, what stands out is the opportunity to see other people in person. This lets us talk with them face-to-face before and after the service.

When the meeting ends, few people leave. We linger and talk, albeit mostly with an awkward, socially distanced gulf separating us. Still, it's much-needed interaction that we want to enjoy for as long as we can. I'm excited to be with some of my church community again, albeit a limited subset. I don't want to leave.

In a week and a half, we'll build on these two trial runs to hold an outdoor Sunday church service. I expect Sunday will have a much better attendance than these two midweek meetings, which vied with limited but competing schedules and the allure of other outdoor activities.

Takeaway: Seek ways to facilitate in-person interaction—especially during challenging circumstances—to foster communication and support much-needed spiritual interaction.

A Holiday Weekend

Sunday, July 5, 2020

We now have experienced two midweek outdoor services. This heightens my anticipation of what is coming, and I chafe at the need to wait another week to experience in-person community on a Sunday.

A nearby church, however, has been holding outdoor services for a few weeks, with one scheduled for today. In a move partially borne out of impatience and partially out of rebellion, Candy and I head there to experience their outdoor service.

It's a warm summer day with an 80-degree temperature and 65 percent humidity. An occasional gentle puff of wind offers some relief, but not enough. I intended to bring sunscreen but forgot. Fortunately, we find space under the protective shelter of a shade tree. Not all are so fortunate, baking in the sun the entire service. Because of the uncomfortable humidity, they promise a shorter service.

Here they have no expectation of staff or attendees wearing masks. And though they encourage social distancing, most people treat it as a suggestion more than a rule. This doesn't bother me. I'm thrilled to be around other people. I so need it.

The opening segment of the service lasts fifteen minutes. In this time, we read Psalm 95, sing two choruses, and hear announcements and an opening prayer. The 25-minute sermon links the United States' Independence Day, which was yesterday, to Israel's Independence Day as remembered through the Passover celebration. Moving ahead in the biblical narrative, the minister connects Passover with Communion that celebrates Jesus's sacrifice and subsequent resurrection.

We sing a concluding song and the service ends. Though some people acknowledge us at a distance with a wave or a smile, the only person who talks to us is a neighbor and then just briefly. The experience of meeting with other Christians to acknowledge our common faith fills me, yet the lack of meaningful interaction with other people counters that feeling. I leave ambivalent about the experience. Overall, this service neither delighted nor disappointed me. It's an all-too-familiar impression that happened more often than it should have during our *52 Churches* and *More Than 52 Churches* sojourns.

We head home to celebrate the holiday weekend with our daughter and her family. This stands as the highlight of my day.

* * *

Later, I watch our church's 50-minute service online. Though I typically watch it on Vimeo, this time I check out the Facebook feed. This is because for the last couple of weeks, they've been chatting live during the service. Though it seems like a disconnect, our associate pastor, who speaks via a recorded message, also heads up the online chat. This is possible because of the time-shifting wonder of technology. His recorded message and live chat are concurrent.

Though it's too late for me to take part in the chat, I read what others have said. As the service begins, several people announce their presence in chat or give a generic welcome to everyone else. After this initial flurry of activity, no one aside from our associate pastor makes another entry for the rest of the service. He responds to some of the initial chat communications and leaves comments about key aspects of his message, which is from Luke 11:24–26.

In one post, he gives the essential element of his talk, "This is a season of removal . . . but after the process of removal, what do we fill it with?" He later shares a quote from Blaise Pascal: "There is a God-shaped vacuum in the heart of every person which cannot be filled by a created thing, but only by God, the Creator, made known through Jesus."

A worship team of five leads us in a couple of songs, and our associate pastor gives the benediction via a wrap-up video. In chat, he concludes with a reminder of next Sunday's service.

Though the opening shot comes from the home of our students' director, all the others take place on a stage at our founding church's facility. For his segments, our minister stands alone on an empty stage, with his words reverberating through an empty theater. The worship set, recorded at a different time, is on the same stage, this time with all the team's instruments and equipment filling the space.

Using a church facility for part of the service reminds me we're inching back toward normal, with church staff allowed to return to their offices and not restricted to working from home. I appreciate the symbolic suggestion that this subtle shift in environment signals, but I miss the intimacy of each participant recording their segment from their home, which better resonates with me. It's a more personal connection, albeit at a distance.

I wish we had started our outdoor service today and not delayed another week. But they chose not to launch our first Sunday service on a holiday weekend. I understand the reason but question if it was necessary.

Except for Christmas and Easter, our church experiences a drop in attendance on holiday weekends. They put forth less effort on these Sundays. Though the expected elements of the service exist—music and message—their scaled-back service somehow feels less than.

This begs the question of causality. Is the attendance drop a result of the service being simpler, or is the scaling back because fewer people show up? Leadership may claim the second reason, while I worry that the first feeds into it, resulting in a self-fulfilling prophecy of lower attendance on holiday weekends.

Takeaway: Examine your church's expectations and practices on holiday weekends. Do you cut back or pause normal programming because you expect fewer people, or do you proceed with a business-as-usual attitude? If you scale back, do attendees view it as a secondary effort and decide to skip?

Perspectives of Online Church

Questions 5 and 6

The next two sets of questions in the survey explored what people disliked and liked about online church.

Question 5. What do you dislike about online church? (check all that apply)

Lack of connection with others: 76.3%

No pre-church or post-church
interaction: 44.7%

No fellowship time: 43.4%

It's hard to sing along when I'm home: 36.8%

Too many distractions at home:	31.6%
Technology issues:	30.3%
Other:	23.7%

We can generalize the top three responses to this question—a lack of connection with others, no pre-church or post-church interaction, and no fellowship time—as a void of community. Interestingly, at most churches these elements occur outside the planned service.

Other comments:

- Bad acoustics and unbalanced sound because of interferences or technological issues.

- Can't do face-to-face Sacraments of Reconciliation and not able to receive the Holy Eucharist.

- God created us for relationship.

- I can't partake in the sacraments.

- I tried online church once, and it felt very impersonal.

- I'm usually in my PJs. It's not the same as going to church. I miss the connection with my brothers and sisters. I miss singing praises to God with friends.

- It feels just like the countless Zoom meetings I do at work.

- We do our own devotions at home. We are considering house church with a few others.

- It makes the isolation much worse.

- It's easy to not watch.

- You can't meet and fellowship in person with other Christians to discuss issues that have occurred during the week.

- It's difficult to know the less-than-obvious things going on in the life of the local church, as well as the lives of others that attend with me.

- I miss being inspired and encouraged by the worship of others.

- My faith tradition is one where we receive the Lord's Supper as a sacrament: the body and blood of our Lord and Savior Jesus Christ. I can't do that online.

- My Wi-Fi is sometimes slow, making it hard to understand sign language.

- Too much screen time is bad for your eyes.

- You cannot make eye contact.

- It is more difficult to be flexible with the agenda.

Question 6. What do you like about online church? (check all that apply)

Accessible any time:	56.8%
Convenient:	48.7%
No need to dress up or look presentable:	41.9%

No need to drive to church: 39.2%

No difficult conversations or
uncomfortable social interactions: 17.6%

I feel free to take part anyway
I want without others judging me: 16.2%

Fewer distractions at home
than at church: 6.8%

Other: 25.7%

The top two items both address flexibility. People can attend online whenever they want, according to their schedules. This is the opposite of in-person church where people must attend at the stated time, according to the church's schedule.

The next three elements—no need to dress up or look presentable, drive to church, or endure difficult conversations—all relate to the ease of participation.

Additional comments:

- Because I'm not seeing any of the other members of the congregation, the online service feels more like the message and rituals are specifically for me.

- There are more faith-formation and growth opportunities available that hadn't existed pre-pandemic or were too far away or time restrictive. I feel like the pandemic has blessed me with a season of spiritual growth.

- We can listen to a message or pastor that my kids understand better and enjoy.

- The chat feature helped me connect with other Christians in my area and around the world.

- I am glad it became available, but I'm not a fan.

- I can watch in my PJs, anytime.

- I can avoid awkward conversations, like why I don't come more often.

- I find it easier to focus on the message.

- In person, it's hard to express myself with uplifted hands or movements in a packed church, as I want to respect the personal space of those around me.

- I enjoy being able to comment out loud to my spouse and engage in conversation about what we hear.

- I only like it when I am sick or there is a reason I can't go in person.

- My church, which is small, meets through Zoom, so it is more of a virtual gathering than a recorded service.

- None.

- Nothing.

- Safer to stay home than to take my immuno-suppressed son to a space where not everyone wears a mask.

- There is nothing I like about online church. If that becomes my only option, I will not go. There's no point.

Takeaway: Look for ways to correct the weaknesses of your online viewing options. Then seek to apply these insights to enhance your in-person gatherings too.

First Outdoor Service and Online

Sunday, July 12, 2020

Anticipation builds as we get closer to the weekend and our first outdoor Sunday church service approaches. Though it doesn't dampen my expectations, the messaging has changed—or at least my perception of it—from "masks optional" to "masks recommended."

Going forward, our outdoor services will be in the spacious yard of one of our attendees, just down the street from where we used to meet each Sunday. Across the road is parking at the library. Few spots remain open when we arrive fifteen minutes early. We scoot into one of the last spaces, grab our lawn chairs, and hike across the lot toward the people congregating for the outdoor service.

A curious passerby asks, "What's going on?"

"An outdoor church service," I say with my most engaging smile.

He nods and continues walking.

"Feel free to join us," I say. I doubt he heard me but pray that one Sunday he'll check out our service.

Candy and I approach the buzz of activity, as volunteers attend to last-minute details and an enthusiastic team of greeters welcomes everyone. Though I recall few attendees with masks at our two midweek services, today about half the people wear them. I feel awkward and squirm a bit, wondering how necessary a mask is when you're outside *and* socially distanced. I suspect it matters little, but for some people it may offer a sense of safety.

During the week, on my daily walks through our neighborhoods, few people wear masks, but most give wide passage to anyone they meet. Strangely, some people also avoid eye contact, as if looking at someone makes them susceptible to the virus.

Today, while a couple of people likewise avert their eyes, most are excited, albeit with a socially distant gap. It's great to see the faces of people we haven't seen for a long time, as well as half of the faces of those wearing masks.

I'm dismayed that I can't identify some of these people—who look vaguely familiar—without also seeing their nose and mouth. I say hi, smile, and give a downward tip of my head. If they respond with a smile, I don't know because it's hidden. If they respond with words, I can't hear because we're too far apart.

Few of the people present have a good understanding of six feet. While a few people disregard it or think six feet is more like four, most people err toward the opposite extreme, standing ten to twelve feet away from others. It's hard to carry on a conversation at that distance, especially when a mask muffles their words and outdoor noises vie for our attention.

Still, we're around other people, and it feels so good. Though an online service accomplishes the tangible expectations of a church service, it falls far short in connecting with others. I now realize, more fully than ever, how essential it is to be in Christian community. I've not had this in months, and only now do I realize the deep void its absence has inflicted on my soul.

A nearby church is also holding an outdoor service at the same time. Though we can't hear them, I later learn they could hear us.

To signal that the service is about to start, the worship team plays. I feel it's louder than needed, and I wonder what the neighbors on either side of us think. Will they experience church with us today from their homes, or will they curse us for interrupting their Sunday-morning slumber?

The meeting follows our typical format, mirroring the experience of our midweek ramp-up preparation services. Since we're a portable church that meets at the local school, our teams excel at setting up for church each week. This requires that someone assembles every aspect of our Sunday experience before the service and disassembles and repacks it afterward. With many hands, it doesn't take long.

After a warm welcome and announcements, we sing songs and listen to a message—just like at our other pre-pandemic services. Aside from being outside, however, nothing about the service seems noteworthy. What stands out is us gathering and having the potential to interact with each other in person.

The service concludes. We pack up our lawn chairs and linger to talk, though few others seem open to doing so.

The few interactions we have are brief and from afar, with no significance other than a basic level of friendliness. With Candy at my side, I try to adopt the most approachable posture I can muster. Still, no one—neither masked nor unmasked—seems interested. At last, a masked friend looks at me, all the while staying about fifteen feet away.

We lock eyes. I suspect she's saying something, but I hear nothing and can't see if her mouth is moving.

I smile, wave, and say, "Have a great week."

She's still looking at me, but I don't know if she responded.

I wave again, repeat myself, and turn to catch up with Candy, who's already ambling toward our car.

It was good to be *around* people, but I leave lonely, dragging a foreboding emptiness with me. For all my anticipation of being here, I completely missed out on making meaningful connections.

* * *

Not everyone, however, joined us for the outdoor service. For those uncomfortable with a face-to-face gathering or unable to attend, the church offered an online version as well. This is not a recording of the outdoor service but a separate production, following their practice of the past several months. The thirty-nine-minute recording starts with a three-minute countdown timer. The first video is of our pastor giving a welcome and reminding everyone that there's also an outdoor service.

Without a Scripture reading or opening prayer, he launches into his message. It's the same content, albeit shorter, that he gave at our outdoor service. He concludes with a blessing.

The next shot is of our worship team. A crew of five leads us through the worship set. I suspect it's the same songs as for the outdoor service, but I'm not sure.

The service ends with a sendoff from our pastor. I think it's a repeat of what they've used in prior weeks. It's practical to not reproduce what already exists, and it makes sense for them to reuse prior clips. It's an efficient use of time, but I feel slighted. I wonder how many times I've seen this same video without realizing it was a rerun. This is a reminder of how easy it is for me to tune out a service's conclusion.

A recording of another staff member gives a last goodbye and sends us out into our week.

Once we have put this ordeal behind us and return to meeting in person, may we remember that other people will still be absent. This could be because of their work situation, physical limitations, or health issues. When we again meet in person, let's not forget the rest of our church who aren't there but still need connection.

Takeaway: Providing service options, especially during times of uncertainty, is a smart move to meet the needs of as many people as possible.

Canceled / Not Canceled

Sunday, July 19, 2020

With our second Sunday outdoor service scheduled for this weekend, I wake to an unexpected email. Due to predicted weather conditions, the outdoor service has been canceled. Fortunately, the online version is in place and will be ready to go at 10 a.m. as usual.

This is possible only because they've opted not to record or stream the outdoor service, instead continuing to produce the needed segments of the online version earlier in the week, making it separate from and not dependent on what happens Sunday morning.

Though they canceled one option, the other will proceed as planned. I applaud their foresight.

For those who intend to watch online, nothing will change. Those who plan to *go* to church, however, must adjust. The simple solution is to stay home and watch online as we've done for the past five months.

Though I appreciate them exercising caution in attempting to hold an outdoor service when rain threatens, I wonder if they gave up too soon or too easily. The church down the street, where we visited two weeks ago, makes the opposite decision. They don't cancel their outdoor service. Candy and I go there instead of staying home and watching online.

The weather, it turns out, isn't an issue.

There's always a risk with outdoor services, as the weather will do whatever it wants. If the outdoor stage sits in a protected area or can have an overhead awning, the items of worship, especially electronic gear, face minimal threat from rain. Without this protection from the elements, however, I understand their desire to cancel the service, even though I don't embrace their decision.

Though I've been to many outdoor services, sometimes in less-than-pleasant conditions, this is only the second time I recall one being canceled. (The other was Church #15: An Outlier Congregation in *52 Churches*—though in that case the outdoor service simply moved inside.)

Even indoor services sometimes face cancellation. This may be because of a problem with the facility, such as a water issue, power outage, or no heat. Over the years, I've encountered all three. These changes in plans relate mostly to issues of comfort, determined on a case-by-case basis.

Other cancellation concerns occur over the weather. In our area these include inclement winter weather and tornado watches and warnings. In these instances, it's an issue of personal safety. Some churches have established policies to guide them on when to call off a service, how to notify attendees, and what contingency plans they have.

Takeaway: Canceling a church service is a tricky decision that requires balancing multiple, sometimes conflicting, considerations. Having a policy in place helps guide the decision. Informing attendees about the criteria, how they'll receive notification, and backup options helps them best deal with the situation when a cancellation must occur.

The Dog Days of Summer

July 26–August 30, 2020

A s we move forward, I realize I need a Sunday church experience where interaction can take place. With some churches resuming indoor Sunday services, we seek them out, going to the outdoor church service down the street the other weeks. We continue in this mode through the summer.

We go to church a couple of times with our daughter and her family. We've been there several times pre-pandemic. Now they've increased the spacing between rows to six feet apart, disinfect between services, and encourage social distancing. With many regulars opting to stay home, and, I assume, watch online, in-person attendance is down. There is an airy, comfortable feel. We enjoy the opportunity to talk with others before and after the service.

We also visit a large area church. We're there for their second in-person gathering after reopening. Their website lists extensive protocols they'll follow. These include taking our temperature at the entrance, conducting a health survey before letting us enter, and practicing social distancing throughout. I'm surprised when none of these occur once we arrive, though they have blocked off every other row in the sanctuary.

People pack into many of the open rows, with no regard to leaving space between family units. The main floor has little room for more people, though from what I can tell the balcony sits empty. When the service ends, people flood toward the exits, giving no thought to their proximity to others. We hold back for a time but eventually follow. I'm not critical of the disconnect between their stated policy and actual practice as much as I'm amused by it. We're not put off by this and return for a second visit.

The church down the street is between ministers. At each outdoor service we hear a different speaker. Some messages are good, leaving us thought-provoking ideas to take home and contemplate, while other sermons are hard to follow, providing few meaningful moments. Though we seldom arrive early enough for much pre-church interaction, we linger after the service and always talk with at least one person. This reminds me just how much I miss chatting with another person face-to-face.

One common trait with each of these contacts, however, distresses Candy. They're all people she knows through her work as our township clerk. They end up talking about what they have in common: township business. Though her job, in theory, is three days a week, most weeks receive six days of her attention. This leaves Sunday as the one day she doesn't think about work—until people at church bring it up.

Though sometimes the minutia of these conversations bores me, overall, I'm glad to meet people I've only heard about and gain greater insight into my wife's job. Still, it would be nice if someone who didn't know us would come up and introduce themselves.

* * *

Throughout these Sunday wanderings, our church continues with their mask-recommended, socially distanced, outdoor services. Though I applaud their caution, I'm dismayed that they're an outlier and seem out of step compared to our other church experiences during this time.

They also continue with their separately produced online services. I check out some of them but don't notice any changes worth mentioning. I do, however, appreciate one addition to their messaging. They talk about small groups restarting. But they don't mention resuming Breaking Bread, where Candy and I had completed the first of three meetings before pausing the last two.

* * *

It's hard to navigate an ever-changing set of expectations, especially when people possess diverging perspectives on how to proceed. Take care to balance the extremes to find a moderating middle. Looking only at concerns for physical health and safety, complete isolation seems the best solution during a pandemic. However, this sacrifices other human essential needs from a mental, emotional, and spiritual perspective.

It's difficult to determine the right answer, but it is an issue we must wrestle with.

Takeaway: As with most things in life, finding a healthy balance is key. This includes how to best conduct church services and maintain Christian community in uncertain times.

Labor Day Weekend Rerun

Sunday, September 6, 2020

Without a countdown timer, the recording begins immediately with an introduction from our senior pastor. Today they'll repeat a prior service, sharing the opening message of a four-part sermon series. Links to the other three messages appear below the video. He asks us to watch all four messages over this Labor Day weekend.

This online experience for us, however, doesn't occur Sunday morning but Sunday night. When this rerun first aired, we were at the outdoor service up the street. Had I expected our church's online service to offer me fresh content, I'd have been painfully disappointed. Yet I've already heard a sermon—one new to me—and experienced a bit of in-person community as a bonus.

I seldom watch reruns on TV and see no point in watching a repeat of a church service. Candy doesn't object when I stop the video and turn off the television. This reuse of programming isn't possible with in-person services, but it is an option for online.

Later, I'm curious if they repeated the entire service or just the message. I go online to check. Yes, they reposted everything, with the only change being the introduction.

With it being a holiday weekend, this shouldn't surprise me. But it does. Over the years, I've been to too many churches that don't offer their best on holiday weekends, scaling back their programming or tapping their B team to lead the service. It becomes a downward spiral. The reduced effort results in an even lower attendance. This reinforces the leadership's decision to pull back on their service and encourages them to downscale even more.

Church leaders who expect to serve their church community need to offer their best and not recycle old content. Just as a congregation wouldn't tolerate a minister repeating a past sermon in person, they shouldn't do so online either.

Takeaway: If you want people to show up on Sunday, make sure you give them a reason to.

Preferred Online Format

Questions 7 and 8

After inquiring about their likes and dislikes of online church, I asked respondents about the format.

Question 7. Is your online church service the same format as in person?

Yes:	84.2%
No:	15.8%

As I expected, most online church services follow the same format as in person, despite the opportunity to take a fresh look at how churches can enhance their online service with innovations not feasible in person. (Though this seems like a missed opportunity, consider the responses to question 8.)

What is different?

- At first, the recordings came from the pastor and worship leaders' homes. Later in the year it was from the building, where it was the same format as in-person church.

- They have a chat feature with people ready to help if someone has a need.

- It is now, but in the beginning, nobody was together at church. The pastor preached at home. Music was one person at home. I stopped doing online after one time.

- Less music.

- Less singing. Everything is shorter. No early interaction time and little fellowship afterward, which I would consider normal parts of my church's service.

- No audience, drier, not as much life in the sermon. No music.

- No human interaction. It's all virtual. Much of it seems contrived. No natural response or empathy.

- No people, just the minister. No singing or fellowship. Shorter service.

- Online is more informal.

- There are two options offered: one with just the teaching and the other is the full service.

- We attend through Zoom with arrangements to take part as well as possible.

- The segments are recorded individually and merged.

PETER DEHAAN

Question 8. If your online church is a different format, do you like or dislike the differences? Why?

There are no differences:	72.3%
I don't like the differences:	18.5%
I like the differences:	9.2%

In this item, I misaligned the question and response options. Some people skipped it, presumably because there was no difference between their in-person and online services, and the wording of the question seemed to exclude them.

Looking only at the responses of people who had an opinion about the differences, twice as many didn't like them as opposed to those who did. It's a reminder of people's tendency to oppose change.

Why do you feel this way?

- This is a God-given opportunity to reimagine what church could be.

- I learn best and grow most from people and prayer and discussion, not sermons.

- No social interactions.

- It's not that I dislike online, but I miss testimonies and connections. Online is great, but something is missing.

- It's only teaching and no worship music.

- Both are fine with me, because it is still a time to focus on the Lord and receive his word.

- I feel when I go to church, I give that time to God and I focus on doing that. At home, I find it easy to be distracted and lose concentration. Also, my 16-year-old daughter will go with me to church but won't watch a service online.

- I enjoy being at church better.

- I like it. I know every week a lot of effort goes into putting everything together. They never ask for money.

- I like the differences but still miss being in the same room with others worshiping Jesus.

- I miss that our children cannot have Sunday school. That's the biggest difference.

- I really miss the children's ministry and think it's crucial for a church to instruct the children at their level.

Takeaway: Dismiss the easiest way to produce online content and explore the *best* option to engage an online audience and invite them into greater participation with your congregation.

Transitioning into Fall

Tuesday, August 18, 2020

Prior to the pandemic, our church rented space from the local school for our Sunday gatherings. Our state's governor, however, mandated that public schools may no longer rent their facilities, at least through January 2021. Most people I've talked with expect her to extend this moratorium, even making it permanent. This means our portable church needs to find a new place to meet.

Fortunately, a top-notch banquet facility is not far away. In the past, we've met there for special occasions, such as Christmas and a few isolated Sundays when the school was not available because of maintenance issues.

Starting in the fall, September 13, this banquet facility will be our new place to meet "for the foreseeable future."

Our senior pastor shares this information, via video, from a familiar setting: the enclosed deck on the back of his house. It's a most comfortable spot. He's used this setting many times over the last six months to record his portions of the Sunday service and other important communications. It feels like he's invited me into his home to share this news with me personally.

Over the summer, he's communicated with many people and held focus groups to determine the best way to move forward. He acknowledges that no one-size-fits-all solution exists, and whatever they decide to do won't work for everyone. Some people will, understandably, not like the results.

Just as they've done throughout the summer, they'll continue offering both in-person and online opportunities for Sunday services. The only change is swapping out an outdoor service, which will soon be an unacceptable option because of the approaching fall and winter, for an indoor setting at the banquet facility.

With this transition, new safety protocols will be in place. These include wearing a mask inside the facility and throughout the service, social distancing—with spaced-out seating, cleaning between services, and changing the order of worship to further minimize health risks.

They'll also resume Sunday-morning children's programming, but they're still working out the details. The video includes a link to an online survey to gather the needed information so they can plan what Sunday-morning children's ministries will look like and how to best move forward.

Regardless, the goal is to create a great in-person worship experience for as long as possible.

During this time, they'll continue to offer online options, just as they've done since the pandemic started. Instead of producing a separate video for the online portion, however, they hope to livestream the in-person service. Throughout this, they'll follow the practice of the local school, which offers both online and in-person learning opportunities for students. Implicitly, if the school pulls back to online learning only, they'll follow their lead and adopt an online-only service for that season.

Acknowledging that there haven't been many ways for us to connect with others throughout this ordeal, they'll offer new online opportunities in the fall for relational connection, such as launching groups for Bible study and discipleship.

During this season, many have pulled away. Our pastor acknowledges that, despite all the connection options currently available—outdoor service, online service, and house church/home church worship—only about one third of us regularly connect using *any* of them. This suggests that two-thirds of the people connect with none of these options or do so infrequently.

Now is the time to lean in, to reconnect and reengage, instead of leaning back.

Takeaway: Planning, especially during times of ever-changing uncertainty, is key. Effectively communicating these plans may be even more important. Explain them with care and explain often.

In-Person at Last—or Not?

Sunday, September 13, 2020

"Join us this Sunday," the email reads. "We will hold two [indoor] worship services every Sunday at 9 a.m. and 10:30 a.m." I'm both excited and hesitant. One thing I learned about myself over the past six months of pandemic protocols is that health and safety procedures thwart effective interaction. I simply can't communicate with someone when we're standing six feet apart and both wearing masks. I guess at more words than I can hear, and I assume the same for them. For me, the effective result of going to church in person means that I won't experience any significant community. I may as well stay home and watch online—or not.

We discuss this with our son and daughter-in-law. Pre-pandemic, we went to church with them every Sunday, along with their two children. Now they have three. Their pediatrician advises them to keep their newborn home and away from nonfamily.

We haven't seen them as much as we've wanted over the past half year, and church could offer the opportunity to connect. But since they won't be returning at this time, neither will we. Instead, we'll go to church this Sunday with our daughter, son-in-law, and their children. With the relaxed expectations there, we'll be able to talk with others before and after the service. I so need that connection.

* * *

Later in the day I look for the recording of our church's in-person service on Facebook, but I can't find it. I assume they met, but I'm not sure.

Searching later in the day, I find a link to the special online version on Vimeo. I wonder if they had technical issues in trying to record the in-person service or if it wasn't their plan to do so this week. Fortunately, their online version is available to share the message and the music, just as they have done in past months.

On Monday, I see an audio link for the service posted on Facebook.

Takeaway: Technology problems can interfere with a planned church service. Having a backup is a wise precaution.

Providing Options

Sunday, September 20, 2020

This week, I again can't find a link to the in-person service on Facebook, but it gives a link to the service on Vimeo. On Monday they add a link on Facebook to an audio recording of the message, now available on the church's website.

Despite not being able to offer the actual in-person church service, they provide two online options: one via video and the other audio only.

Takeaway: Providing options for people to connect online is a smart solution when they can't meet in person.

Livestream at Last

Sunday, September 27, 2020

Up to this point, our church's online services have been custom content created for an online experience. I'm eager to compare this with them streaming an in-person service. At last, I can. Though I've experienced streaming from other churches, now I can contrast our custom-produced content with a livestream.

This Sunday I find a link to our church's in-person service. I'm not sure if this is the first week they posted the service online or merely the first time I've found it. Regardless, I'm excited to watch. I yearn to experience a "normal" service—albeit from afar.

This is something I haven't been able to do with our church in seven months.

I applaud their ongoing efforts at providing meaningful Sunday experiences each week. But watching a video of an actual service feels like moving one step closer to reclaiming what once was.

The video starts with a shot of our worship team who open with a song. The service proceeds as usual: an initial worship set, announcements and opening prayer, message, concluding worship set, and blessing to send us on our way. Though they said they would tweak the order of the service to better align with pandemic protocols, I don't see a difference.

When the first service is over, a series of informational slides cycle through, repeating for the next thirty minutes, as we wait for the second service to begin. I like this approach because viewers who want to make sure they can connect before the service starts will see these slides to let them know they're in the right place.

As the time to start the second service draws near, background music begins, alerting us that something's about to happen. In a few minutes, the repeating slides give way to a welcome message and then the worship team appears. The next sixty minutes repeat the first service.

To wrap up the morning, our pastor gives a closing blessing. When he says "amen," a window pops up on the screen for viewers to click a link to receive an alert whenever the church goes live. This is a most helpful option.

The instrumental portion of the worship team plays as people exit the facility. Then the livestream ends, having lasted two hours and forty-four minutes.

They shot the entire video from one fixed camera in the back of the facility. Set to cover the entire stage, it works for both the worship team and the minister. But there was no zooming or panning, no variations in shots the entire time.

A little more disconcerting, however, was that the audio was at a low level, especially for the first service, and not the best quality. For part of the service, I was at full volume and still couldn't hear well.

A third production topic is lighting. Our church services have always occurred under subdued lighting. This provides a worshipful experience—though at times challenging for notetakers. A dimly lit room, however, doesn't display well on video, which requires spotlights for the best quality shots.

If the goal of a viewer is to connect with their church's live meeting and experience a service as they used to, then today's simple livestream smartly accomplishes this. If, however, they expected to see a professionally created video production, the experience would have disappointed them.

These two opposing perspectives highlight a chasm between church attenders who appreciate God-focused simplicity and those who bring a consumer mindset to their Sunday practices.

Indeed, the mantra at many churches once was—and may still be—excellence in all things. Though there's a reason to give our best to God, especially in our Sunday morning services, there's a risk in taking this to an unhealthy extreme.

I recall a friend's experience being on a worship team at a large church with a highly produced service. Each week the worship leader would instruct the vocalists at what point in each song they were to raise their arms in praise of God. When she countered that she preferred to do so as led by the Holy Spirit, her leader rebuffed her and said that was unacceptable.

For our online church services, we must balance the simplicity of a single, fixed camera with the much more professional results accomplished by churches who have been posting services online for years.

There is a world that doesn't know Jesus. If they encounter our online church service, will they dismiss us as a laughable, second-rate experience that's out of touch with today's expectations? Or will our professional production draw them in and point them to Jesus?

While we shouldn't view a church service as entertainment or with the eye of a critic, we are equally wrong to accept any effort—regardless of quality—just because it's offered with sincerity. This is a dilemma each church must grapple with and fully address so they can best advance the kingdom of God.

As for the service I just watched, I applaud their inaugural effort. I know they will continue to tweak it each Sunday, just as they've done with their custom online productions since the pandemic started.

In contrasting our church's custom-produced content from the first part of the pandemic with the livestream offering now, I realize I have different expectations for the two.

I compare custom content to the informal, personal videos I see on social media, especially Facebook and YouTube. This includes YouTubers. Our church's efforts surpass comparable content online that come from non-church sources. It's a comfortable, engaging experience.

For a livestream, I liken it to a television production, as it seems the most similar. At the very least, the standard of comparison is the highly produced and professional output of megachurches and leading parachurch ministries. In this respect, our livestream falls short. Though it may satisfy a regular attendee, a visitor will quickly bounce to something with a higher production value, be it another church service or something more mainstream.

* * *

One of my first jobs was as an audio engineer at a television station. I later applied the lessons learned there when I served on my church's tech team, running the soundboard or operating a camera. I did this under the supervision of a man whose day job was head engineer at another television station.

Here are my thoughts about the audio/visual technology used for online church services:

Audio: Most churches today have an audio system in their facility. Sometimes this is to fill sound in the back portion of the room, as people sitting in the front hear fine without it. In other instances, the sound system mixes the audio for the entire space. Without it, no one would hear much of anything. In both cases, the person at the audio console adjusts levels for what works best for the *room*.

This may or may not be what's best for *online*.

In the first scenario, where the sound system is for fill, the output of the audio board may not work well for a remote feed. An alternative is using a microphone—either built-in or external—to feed directly into the camera. How well this works will depend on the quality of the microphone and its signal level. Experiment with various configurations to determine the best solution.

In the second scenario, the sound system covers the entire sanctuary. Pulling an auxiliary feed from the soundboard may produce the best results. Again, experimentation is essential.

In either case, tapping a professional audiovisual contractor may be the wise approach to produce the best outcome.

Video: The simplest solution for video is a fixed, unmanned camera. Set it up, turn it on, and you're good to go. This static shot, however, will not engage viewers.

The next step is to have a camera operator who can pan and zoom as appropriate. The key word is *appropriate*. Some beginners, enamored with the camera's options, try to use its features continuously. This is too much and too often. Zoom in and pull back only when it makes sense to do so. Pan when there's a good reason for it. Don't be like the one novice camera operator I worked with who zoomed in and followed the offering plate as it weaved its way through the congregation.

Having a second camera gives a variation in shots, but—unless it's a fixed camera—this requires a second operator. With two cameras, however, comes the need for a third person to run a video switcher. With many cameras—some churches have a half dozen or more—another person acts as the producer, instructing the camera operators and video switcher what to do. As you can see, the amount of volunteer staff needed for a more engaging video experience can balloon quickly. Though you may initially have a nice list of eager volunteers, over time their enthusiasm will waver, and they'll move on to other activities that interest them more.

Given this, with remotely operated cameras, one skilled person *might* possess the ability to set up each shot and switch between different cameras to produce a professional and seamless video feed. This takes skill to learn and practice to master. It's unlikely, however, that someone doing this a few Sundays a month for an hour or two will reach this level of proficiency. Regardless, it's an option to consider, or at least move toward.

Takeaway: When streaming a service online, give proper attention to the audio and video quality of the production. Balance the competing extremes of "good enough" and trying to rival a broadcast-quality production by considering your audience, goals, budget, and volunteer pool.

Back to One In-Person Service

Friday, November 20, 2020

On Friday, we receive an email message from our church. Starting this Sunday, the in-person service options will go from two times down to one at 9:30 a.m. They'll continue offering some children's programming during this time.

The message gives no reason for this consolidation, but I assume it's because there aren't enough people attending in-person to justify two services, and that one time will accommodate all who show up. I wonder, however, if the impetus for this doesn't come from the email I received yesterday, saying that a person attending one service last Sunday subsequently tested positive for Covid-19.

Because of HIPAA privacy regulations, they can't provide any other information. This leaves me wondering if this person was at the service Candy and I attended or the other one. And if they were at the same service, were they anywhere near us?

Of course, I'll never know. But given the social distancing and mask requirement, I'm not concerned—at least not too much.

This was only the second service we've been to this fall in person at our church, the rest of the time either watching online or going somewhere else. I only recall talking to one person last Sunday. He served on the tech team that day, taking a break between services. Sitting off by himself, I approached him, and we talked. I remained six feet away from him—almost—and had my mask on. His mask dangled around his neck. This didn't concern me. Once he realized it, he apologized and lifted his mask to cover his mouth and nose.

Though our church's pandemic response felt unnecessarily cautious to me—especially compared to what some other churches were doing—I'm now glad they were overly careful.

Takeaway: When dealing with unprecedented situations, balance precaution with practicality. Then provide open and honest communication to those impacted by your decisions.

~

Plans Change

Thursday, December 3, 2020

On Thursday we receive an email from church—a now-common occurrence—with a link to a video about changes in Sunday's worship plan. The email gives no other information. I presume this is intentional because communication by video is more effective than communication via email.

Obviously, I'm curious. I click the link.

The video, from our senior pastor, shares that, starting next Sunday, they will no longer offer kids programming or hospitality services. Since they never resumed coffee and cookies when they restarted meeting in person, the only hospitality service I'm aware of is greeters at the doors to the building and into the worship area. Aside from the kids programming, which I understand not too many families used, this doesn't seem like a major change.

Though they'll continue to meet in person and stream the service online, the reason for scaling back the amenities is that the number of in-person attendees has decreased as the number of positive cases in our state has increased. Most people attending in person are those serving or related to someone serving.

They will continue in this mode until further notice. Given the speed and necessity of changes we've endured the last eight months, "further notice" could last only a couple of weeks or could drag on for a few months.

Change is unsettling, and we've endured frequent and jarring change through most of the year—both in our personal lives and in our church community. Yet when conditions shift, change is the wise action.

It's foolish to persist in maintaining the status quo when there's no longer a justification for it.

Takeaway: Pursue change when there's a good reason to do so. Balance the impulse to try something new with the human tendency to resist it.

Closed Captioning

Sunday, January 10, 2021

I don't know if it's been there before and I missed it, but today I spot a closed captioning option on the Facebook feed. (Closed captioning isn't available on the Vimeo recording.) Curious, I turn it on. During the opening song, the lyrics appear as usual, but there's no closed captioning. Maybe it doesn't work for singing. As soon as the music ends and the worship leader begins talking, his words appear at the bottom of the screen.

The text continues to display as he makes the hand-off to our associate pastor. He gives the welcome and thanks all the volunteers, specifically the tech team for their efforts to deal with problems and make everything work. Ironically, the video has cut out a couple of times, although the audio continues without interruption. After about five minutes, they resolve the video feed issue, and it works fine for the rest of the service. Such are the risks when streaming a service live.

Today is Communion. For those watching online, our associate pastor instructs us to round up what we can at our home to represent the Communion elements: the bread and the juice. After announcements, he prays and delivers today's message. It's shorter than usual. He finishes, the worship team returns for their second set, and we celebrate Communion as a community. Then the worship team returns for their third set to wrap up the service.

Throughout the hour-long recording, closed captioning works perfectly sometimes and doesn't work at all other times. Sometimes, after a period of displaying nothing, the words speed by, trying to catch up, but I suspect some sections never do appear.

* * *

There are two types of closed captioning. The traditional approach occurs between taping and broadcast, where a person listens to the recording and manually types the words. However, someone with quick and accurate typing skills can do this live, producing closed captioning in near real time. This introduces a slight delay, but it's normally not an issue.

As with many things, technology has advanced to a point where it can handle closed captioning too, albeit not as good as a person—at least not yet. Doing so uses voice-to-text technology.

I'm familiar with voice-to-text software, as I use it to write. I often dictate my words instead of typing them. I've done this for a couple of years and the technology keeps getting more accurate. Despite my less-than-ideal diction, it works well enough for me.

The same speech-to-text technology increasingly produces closed captioning for low-budget television and movie productions, as well as for live events. Its speed and accuracy hinges on two elements. One is receiving an audio signal of sufficient volume and quality. The other is the speaker's enunciation. When both aspects are sufficient, the closed-captioned results are fast and accurate. The only hiccup occurs when it encounters proper names, especially unusual ones, which can turn up when reading the Bible or in sermons. Still, the software makes its best determination on what word to display. Often, it's close enough, though sometimes the results provoke a chuckle.

Closed captioning is another option we can use for our online church services. We could even tap it for our in-person services too, displaying the spoken words on the screen in the sanctuary. This is an example of an online application making its way back to an in-person church service.

Takeaway: As technology evolves, look for ways where it can enhance the experience both online and in person. Don't let the naysayers, the Luddites, dissuade you from moving forward in using new tools to enhance a worship experience and connect with others.

Just because we shift back to an in-person service doesn't mean we have to abandon the good parts of our online offerings. This is especially true if it makes the service more accessible for the disabled or can benefit those on the fringes.

Returning

Sunday, January 24, 2021

L eading up to Thanksgiving, Candy and I guarded our interactions with others, taking extra precautions to limit human contact. We didn't want to risk exposure to the coronavirus and need to cancel our scaled-back Thanksgiving celebration due to quarantine requirements. How we so needed this interaction and the hint of normal. If we had contact with someone who later tested positive, we would need to isolate ourselves for up to two weeks.

After Thanksgiving, we felt free to attend an in-person service. We later received a message that a person in attendance with us tested positive. It was unclear when being in proximity with someone who later test-ed positive resulted in home-based quarantine and when it didn't, but the church issued no such edicts.

Given that, we again opted to stay home and limit our social interactions with others, so as not to risk our scaled-back Christmas and New Year's celebra-tions with family.

Throughout December and continuing into Jan-uary, we attended church online. We didn't go any-where unless it was necessary. This included Candy going to work and getting groceries. Since I work at home, it meant that I stayed sequestered.

* * *

As January winds down, we can't stand it anymore. With apprehension, we venture back to the in-person service at our church. Though the option to attend has been there for the past two months, the official stance encouraged us to stay home and watch online. At last, they loosen that position and invite us to at-tend in person.

With a bit of trepidation, Candy and I return. The attendance is sparse but better than the last time we were here (just after Thanksgiving). The staff, pleasantly surprised we ventured out, are most happy to see us. It feels good to have our presence celebrated. It's exhilarating to see other people in real life. We even enjoy extended conversations after the service. Aside from my small writer's group, these are the first non-family people I've talked with in person in three months.

The next week, our son and daughter-in-law join us with their three kids. With no children's programming, including no nursery, we sit as a family in the back row. It's challenging to occupy three preschoolers, one a newborn. But between us four adults, we keep them engaged and mostly quiet.

What's interesting is that we aren't the only families sitting in the back with infants. After the service, three moms with babies gather. None of them knew the others were expecting; seeing them with young ones is surprising. It's a reminder that though we've been apart, life has gone on. Families have grown. It's just that each family experienced this growth in isolation and not in community.

Takeaway: When meeting in person isn't an option or doesn't happen, seek ways to allow attendees to connect virtually and not wallow in isolation.

Plans to Return

Question 9

The ninth survey question asked about people's plans to return to in-person church once they felt it was safe to do so.

Question 9. What are your plans once it is safe to return to church in person?

Go just as often as before:	85.1%
Unsure:	5.4%
Go more often than before:	4.1%
Look for other church options:	2.7%
Continue to experience church online:	2.7%
Go, but not as often as before:	0.0%

From this select group of respondents, most plan to resume their prior attendance levels once it's safe to do so. Interestingly, a few expect they'll go more often, while none plan to scale back.

Additional comments:

- We watch other churches that do a better job of online service.

- We are now back in church Sunday morning—no Sunday school or Bible studies at church. They are on Zoom, which has worked well.

- I am single, so it is hard going to a new church alone. So many questions, but I will look for a church home again.

- I look forward to connecting with others.

- I'll maybe also do house church or switch over to house church.

- My husband and I have gotten together with other believers, found a pastor, a music group, and a barn [to meet in]. We have been worshiping, hearing the Word of God, and having fellowship every Sunday evening. We have felt strongly that churches should *never* for any reason close their doors. This world needs Jesus more than ever. We have taken the command of Hebrews 10:23–25 literally and seriously, yes, even in a pandemic.

- Our church is meeting in person and has been doing this since summer. We require masks and limit the length of the service. We have no other activities at church. All meetings and Bible studies are on Zoom.

- We are already meeting with caution.

- We are already going back to regular church. Our church offers online services, but we prefer to attend in person.

- We have been attending all along.

- We're already back doing in-person services.

Takeaway: Though we hope that in-person church attendance will eventually return to pre-pandemic numbers, keep in mind that not all people will come back. Some will search for other options and others will continue online. Make sure your website and on-line options are there for them.

One Year In

At the one-year anniversary of our church sending us home for Sunday worship and the effective beginning of the pandemic, I pause at what lies ahead. With expectation, we march toward a new normal, both for society and church specifically.

Yet I question at what point in this journey we will set aside masks and social distancing. We may never get there. Will concern over human touch with casual acquaintances ever fade? Will fist bumps and elbow taps replace the traditional handshake for good? Will we ever return to social interaction and gatherings without giving a thought to its impact on our physical health?

Indeed, as the number of positive cases trend upward in our state, many brace for our governor to mandate another lockdown and send us scurrying back to home-bound isolation.

Regardless of what happens, I know two things.

First, given the church's record over the past year, I know she will adjust to whatever happens. She will provide us with the best way to connect with others and God, whether at church as it once was, in-person under a new normal, or at home and connecting online.

Second, I don't know what the future holds. No one does—except for God. I turn what will be over to him and trust him to provide for us as he always has. And with his help, I'll do my best to not worry about the future.

May we all embrace him for who he is. Amen.

An Online Discussion about Online Church

As I sought input from others about online church, we did so virtually, exchanging emails or using online chat. As expected, most people I interacted with opposed online church, sometimes vehemently. Some of this negative reaction comes from the normal human tendency to oppose change, although many people gave good reasons to support their perspectives.

These include a lack of connection and fellowship, not being able to sing in community, and a profound sense of loss.

Acknowledging these concerns, Carol Forbes, however, also sees the positive. "I am just happy that I can still have the Word of God preached and join my church family virtually," she says. She also acknowledges the benefit of having a church experience from home when she isn't feeling well. Even so, "I can't wait to get back to church—not the building but the fellowship of being with other children of God."

Many cited this flexibility, with a few admitting to watching online church in bed when they didn't feel like getting up. Michael Roberto also appreciates this option when he is sick, glad for the opportunity to have a spiritual experience online even though he finds watching church on a small laptop screen frustrating.

Even worse is watching on a smart phone or other handheld device. For those with large screen televisions or monitors, screen size isn't a concern. But we must remember that not everyone has this technology in their homes. Close-up shots work well on small screens, but these might be too big on larger displays.

Another person applauding online church flexibility is Sharon Williams. But she's also concerned that it could be too easy to stay home and watch on-line instead of returning to in-person church.

"It's a blessing that we have this option for these challenging times," Beth Foreman adds. "I have appreciated the option to stay safe at home and still take part in a kind of worship. I have even worshiped later with other churches I may never have visited before. So that's a bonus."

Patricia Robertson adds another positive element of an online church service is that it provides her with a sense of connection with her church community. Even so, she finds the internet experience lacking. "It just doesn't feel like church."

Chad Cargill, also not a fan of online church, nevertheless notices an interesting side benefit. He appreciates being able to watch the services of the church he used to attend before moving. With more churches going online, consider how this option may allow you to reconnect with a former faith community for worship, albeit at a distance.

Jenna C. also appreciates the opportunity to experience an array of services through various churches' online offerings, and to explore other "services, traditions, and beliefs." She adds that, collectively, these virtual offerings provide "something for everyone." Though many churches replicate an in-person service online, she most appreciates the "services geared specifically to online audiences."

Robertson says the key to engaging with a livestream service is one of attitude. To sing along and say prayers aloud, even though it's difficult to do at home, helps her—and us—better experience the online service. There is also "the distance factor," she says. "It feels like I'm watching a show rather than participating in a service." As with many people, she looks forward to the day when she can physically return to church.

Though she can't wait to set foot in her church again, Jenna C. adds that she has "very much enjoyed utilizing technology to attend virtual church." Living in a household with high-risk people, she is "thankful that we have this technology available to still feel as though we are part of a faith community, while keeping ourselves safe."

After one year of not attending church in person, she's grateful for "the luxury of access to online church," while also feeling sad, wondering if it will ever be safe enough for her and her high-risk household to return. Though a self-proclaimed introvert who prefers to worship at home and experiences little socialization at church, she still misses the in-person event and can't wait to return. "I look forward to being able to receive the Eucharist," she says.

Foreman also laments not being able to partake of the Lord's Supper. She says it's "life-giving to me for strength and renewal" and "so important to my faith life." But she doesn't see it as an essential element, while noting that for some people it's more critical for them to partake.

"People weren't meant to be islands, nor to be isolated," Sharlene Graf adds. "We need balance." Yet the requirements placed on in-person attendees left her frustrated with social distancing and no singing. Then came the requirement to sign in and sanitize, with person-to-person interaction discouraged. The latest iteration for her in-person experience allows for singing, providing that each person maintains a four-meter buffer (about thirteen feet).

Graf doesn't mention a mandate to wear masks, but this expectation frustrates many people—including myself—because it thwarts effective communication. For some, the mask requirement is enough for them to stay home. Another church performs temperature checks of each attendee before allowing them to enter.

Many people lament the lack of meaningful community, a thought echoed by most people when discussing the downsides of an online church. Though incorporating a chat feature for comments allows for some interaction, most view typing as inferior to talking.

"I don't get to see everyone who is there, as the camera focuses on the priest and other celebrants," says Robertson about online services, but "this is appropriate since it preserves the privacy of those attending." Despite that, she misses seeing everybody.

Amber Lawrence agrees. "I don't like not getting to see [my] church family."

Having an online church community, however, stands as a lifeline for many. It "helped me to not feel as isolated and hopeless," says Jenna C., who appreciates the access afforded by technology.

Not everyone, however, shares this view. "Virtual church represents an option only where there is no physical, local church" says Gabriel. "It undermines collective fellowship and worship. It is not the ideal setting for Christian growth, development, and maturity. It takes away individual responsibility, accountability, transparency, and deprives participants of the spiritual family's experience."

Gabriel notes the command in Hebrews 10:25 to not give up meeting together and to encourage one another. Though some see online church as an acceptable way to meet this requirement, not everyone agrees.

Roberto, a middle-aged single man, laments about his too-frequent difficulties when attending in person, where most churches focus on families and ignore individuals. "They don't know what to do with older singles," he says.

Though we might conclude that online church provides a solution for Roberto and people like him, he sees the same attitudes that made in-person attendance a challenge carried over to the online experience. Still, "we need a physical church family," he says. Online church "wasn't strengthening my faith. It was weakening it."

Several people cited a struggle with distractions when engaging in online church. These can come from both their household and technology, notes Robertson.

Lawrence says, "We have four small children, so we basically get to hear none of the service when we are at home."

Unlike many who struggle with distractions when listening to messages online, however, Jenna C. finds she can better focus on the pastor's message. Robertson also notes that, online, she's able to "focus more on the homily (sermon)."

Viewing the situation from a holistic perspective can help us see big-picture possibilities. "The whole isolation aspect of this pandemic has me thinking more about the elderly, the infirmed, the homeless, and the people left on the sidelines," says Jenna C.

Despite the many benefits and the essential lifeline that online church offers, many can't wait to return to in-person church—without masks—and with singing and hugging. "I cried when I returned to in-person worship," says Foreman. "It meant that much to me."

Williams, along with most others, is "very excited" at the prospect of returning to in-person church.

Given all this, we—both church leaders and laity—should ask, how can the church best meet people's needs in person and online, both during times of pandemic and isolation, as well as after it?

Takeaway: Embrace the diverse opinions about online church and the wisest way to safely meet in person. Though your response won't make everyone happy, seek God as you decide what is wise and will best help the most people.

Online Church Options

In our exploration of online church, the experiences fell into two categories. One was a unique production geared specifically for online viewing. The other was sharing an in-person service online.

Unique Content

What we experienced, especially in the initial days of quarantine, was content created specifically for an online encounter. A series of edited video clips produced an internet-delivered experience and offered a fresh approach to church.

Based on what we were familiar with, these services mirrored many elements of an in-person format: greeting, music, message, and a parting thought.

These elements, however, didn't need to carry any of the constraints of a physical church building. This allowed for creative flexibility and the potential to provide a more meaningful service, accessible from the safety and comfort of viewers' homes.

One element I especially appreciated was discussion questions provided mid-message. We could pause the recording—or not—and explore the topic with those we were meeting with or call someone and discuss it over the phone. We could spend as little or as much time as we wanted to on each question, and the video was waiting for us to resume when we were ready to return to the message, armed with additional insights from our conversation.

I've encountered these mid-message questions a few times at in-person services, but the time allotted for it was either too long or too short for my liking. Those I spoke with during these interludes typically either ran out of things to say, or else we had barely begun our dialogue when the service resumed. This isn't an issue when viewing a service online from home where we control the timing.

I also especially enjoyed clips of non-leaders. These included video greetings, reading Scripture, or sharing part of their story. Though it's an option to integrate video into an in-person service, watching them from home felt more inviting than viewing them in the church sanctuary.

I most enjoyed the variety of settings for each video segment. Having someone talk to me from their home often felt like I was their guest. Though two-way interaction wasn't an option, as a person who listens more than he talks, I didn't mind it at all. The intimacy of these scenes from the various speakers' homes can't happen in an in-person service.

The informal nature of these various clips and the frequent feeling of having a one-on-one conversation removed the need for high-quality production. Yes, we expect a good audio level and a clear image, but beyond that, having a well-honed presentation didn't matter so much. Just as we're used to seeing unpolished personal videos on social media, the same style of custom content for online church is acceptable, even inviting.

Streamed Service

The second, and more common, type of online church we experienced was streaming an in-person event—or at least a representation of one. This is because some of these feeds occurred in the church facility with no audience present.

This option provides attendees the exact format they're familiar with, even if they complain about it or criticize what happened. Staging a replica of an in-person service when people can't enter the building and streaming it online is the easiest way to produce an online church experience.

With this approach, unlike the informal, homey feel that custom content can have, posting a church service online requires a higher standard. People expect a greater level of professionalism, just as if they were watching a concert on TV or viewing a recording of a large conference. This exists as the standard of comparison for most viewers of livestreamed services.

Yes, a church's committed members will accept a solitary, fixed camera shot of the entire service. Occasional attendees, visitors, and those checking out a church, however, will not appreciate this simplistic approach. They'll judge it in comparison to the highly produced output of churches that have been broadcasting their service online for years.

I embrace Pastor Keith Jones's assessment, which we covered earlier, that "streaming is the new front door to church attendance. I don't think people will come in the door who haven't seen us online first."

If a church passes this first screen, then a visitor may decide to dress up, drive to the facility, and muster enough courage to venture inside. Disappoint them online and they'll never show up in person. Though a low-budget, casual approach can be endearing in a custom online experience, this same mentality falls short for most people when viewing an actual church service.

Audio quality is essential, yet too many of the services I experienced online were hard-to-understand. Equally important is video quality. A blurred image won't cut it. Poor lighting will detract. A shot not properly framed will distract.

If a church's online service leaves viewers wanting because of poor audio or video quality, they'll assume the in-person service will likewise disappoint. Yet this may not be the case. I've viewed services online after first attending them in person. What impressed me as a quality experience with professional execution when I sat in the building turned to disappointment when I later watched the same service online.

Setting up a single, fixed camera to capture an in-person church service for online streaming or subsequent posting will fall short for most viewers who expect more. It may be a simple solution, but it's not the right approach.

Virtual Reality

There's a third option. Virtual reality church. The thought may shock some or even seem an anathema to meaningful Christian community or genuine connection, yet it's a possibility, and it exists—right now.

In a television interview—fittingly posted online—Bishop D. J. Soto of Virtual Reality Church (vrchurch.org), said that he didn't set out to create a virtual reality church but that's where God led him. With Soto and his church using virtual reality since 2016, he has much experience in creating a Christian community of believers, spiritual seekers, and the merely curious in cyberspace. He notes that virtual reality is an ideal gathering place for the homebound and those with severe social anxieties, which would prevent them from leaving their house to attend a church service.

For those who haven't had a virtual reality experience, each virtual attendee creates an online avatar for themselves and then enters the virtual church facility. They can interact with the other avatars and hold meaningful conversations.

A worry of some is that behind the façade of an avatar, people will pretend to be someone they aren't, putting up a false front—just as sometimes happens at churches in real life. Soto's experience, however, confirms the opposite. Under the protection of an avatar, people—even those talking to strangers on their first visit—feel comfortable representing themselves honestly and being who they truly are.

I won't say anything more about this futuristic-sounding option here because others already have. With the recent publication of several books about virtual reality church, expect more information to follow.

When you're ready to explore this option further, search for "virtual reality church" to view resources, read information, and discover books on the subject. Even if you aren't ready to take such a bold step, it may be a smart move to learn about virtual reality church now, before it becomes requested or even expected.

Conclusion

Though we might one day return to church as normal and forget about the challenges and opportunities presented by the pandemic, we might never return to what once was. Instead, we'll settle into a new normal. A more fearsome possibility, which I pray will never occur, is that we'll find ourselves permanently restricted from in-person gatherings, with online church becoming our only option.

Regardless of which path the future takes, never forget that some people, for varying reasons, cannot or will not attend church in person. For them, online is the only option. Don't forget these people; continue to seek ways to minister to them.

Takeaway: Regardless of what the future holds, online church—in one form or another—is an option we must pursue. Doing so will enable us to better serve and minister to people who avoid attending church in person for whatever reason.

In addition, having an ongoing, viable online church presence will best position each church for the future, whatever it holds.

Appendix: Churches Covered

Question 10

The final item in the 10-question survey asked respondents to share links to churches they watch online. These congregations range from small to large, from rural to megachurches and multi-location networks. Some receive little acknowledgment for their work and others are well known. They also cover the full gamut of Christianity, from traditional to contemporary, liturgical to non-liturgical, formal to informal. Their online content reflects this beautiful variety.

Of the responses to this question, a few websites no longer work. One is undergoing an overhaul. And several are "unsecure" sites. I'm not including direct links to their YouTube channel or Facebook page—which many respondents provided—just the churches' websites.

I covered several of these churches throughout this book, picking the ones I felt offered the greatest variety and the most potential to deepen our understanding of online church. The rest provided helpful insights and a more holistic view of ministering to people over the internet.

In alphabetical order, these churches are:

- All Shores Wesleyan Church (allshores.org)

- Blue Route Vineyard Community Church (blueroutevineyard.com)

- Calvary Chapel Chino Hills (calvarycch.org)

- Christ the King Catholic Church (ctkcc.net)

- Community Bible Church (cbcpierre.org)

- Elevation Church (elevationchurch.org)

- Ethiopian Evangelical Church of Atlanta (ee-catlanta.com)

- Faith Church (faithishere.org)

- Fennville Assembly of God (fennvilleag.org)

- First Reformed Church (plattefrc.com)

- First Southern (firstsouthern.tv)

- Frontline Community Church (frontlinegr.com)

- Green Lake Calvary Church (greenlakecalvary.org)

- Harvest at Home (harvest.org/at-home)

- Jamestown Harbor Church (jamestownharborchurch.org)

- New Hope Fellowship (newhopefellowship.org)

- North Point Community Church (northpoint.org)

- Northbridge Church (northbridge.cc)

- Northstar Church (northstarknox.com)

- Saint Maximilian Kolbe Parish (stmkp.org)

- Pathway Church (pathwaypeople.org)

- Reclamation Church (reclamationfreemethodist.com)

- Redemption Church (redemptionmi.org)

- Rolling Hills Covenant Church (rollinghillscovenant.com)

- Southeast Christian Church (southeastchristian.org)

- University Heights Baptist Church (uhbc.org)

- University United Methodist Church (universitychurchhome.org)

- Watermark Fort Worth (fwwatermark.org)

- West Kalamazoo Christian Church (westk.org)

- Zion Lutheran (zionholland.com)

[This list is accurate at the time of publication, but it's correctness will degrade over time as churches change their names, close their doors, or alter their on-line presence.]

Takeaway: Be sure that people can find your church online. Though social media may be an easy location to set up and maintain, it's not one that you can control. Instead, a website is the preferred destination. Just make sure it's current, working, and secure.

Acknowledgments

Scott, Ben, Abi, Eric, Gina, and others at Jamestown Harbor Church. You inspire, you teach, and you model Jesus.

My dear newsletter friends who provided invaluable feedback: Patricia, Mike, Sharon, Sharlene, Amber, Jenna, Beth, and Gabriel. Also, online friends Keith and Chad.

All who completed my survey about online church. Since your responses were anonymous, I don't know who you are, but God does. I so appreciate your input, which helped inform this book.

My wife, Candy, and our family, who were a big part of this journey.

My steadfast assistant, Shara Anjaynith Cazon, for freeing up my time so I can write more. Joanna Penn, my book publishing mentor from afar. And Thomas Umstattd Jr.'s mastermind group to keep me moving forward.

My amazing book production team listed in the front of this book.

God, who called—and calls me—me to write for him and advance his kingdom.

About Peter DeHaan

P eter DeHaan wants to change the world one word at a time. His books and blog posts discuss God, the Bible, and church, geared toward spiritual seekers and church dropouts. Many people feel church has let them down, and Peter seeks to encourage them as they search for a place to belong.

But he's not afraid to ask tough questions or make religious people squirm. He's not trying to be provocative, but he seeks truth, even if it makes some people uncomfortable. Peter urges Christians to push past the status quo and reexamine how they practice their faith in every area of their lives.

Peter DeHaan earned his doctorate, awarded with high distinction, from Trinity College of the

Bible and Theological Seminary. He lives with his wife in beautiful Southwest Michigan and wrangles crossword puzzles in his spare time.

A lifelong student of the Bible, Peter wrote the 700-page website ABibleADay.com to encourage people to explore the Bible, the greatest book ever written. His popular blog, at PeterDeHaan.com, addresses biblical Christianity to build a faith that matters.

Connect with him and learn more at PeterDe-Haan.com.

If you enjoyed this book, please leave a review online. Your review will help other people discover this book and encourage them to read it too. That would be amazing.

Thank you.

Books by Peter DeHaan

For an up-to-date list of all Peter's books, go to Peter-DeHaan.com/books.

52 Churches series:

- *52 Churches: A Yearlong Journey Encountering God, His Church, and Our Common Faith*

- *The 52 Churches Workbook: Becoming a Church that Matters*

- *More Than 52 Churches: The Journey Continues*

- *The More Than 52 Churches Workbook: Pursue Christian Community and Grow in Our Faith*

Dear Theophilus series:

- *Dear Theophilus: A 40-Day Devotional Exploring the Life of Jesus through the Gospel of Luke*

- *Dear Theophilus, Acts: 40 Devotional Insights for Today's Church*

- *Dear Theophilus, Isaiah: 40 Prophetic Insights about Jesus, Justice, and Gentiles*

- *Dear Theophilus, Minor Prophets: 40 Prophetic Teachings about Unfaithfulness, Punishment, and Hope*

- *Dear Theophilus, Job: 40 Insights About Moving from Despair to Deliverance*

- *Living Water: 40 Reflections on Jesus's Life and Love from the Gospel of John*

- *Love Is Patient: 40 Devotional Gems and Biblical Truths from Paul's Letters to the Corinthians*

Bible Bios series:

- *Women of the Bible: The Victorious, the Victims, the Virtuous, and the Vicious*

- *The Friends and Foes of Jesus: Explore How People in the New Testament React to God's Good News*

Other books:

- *Jesus's Broken Church: Reimagining Our Sunday Traditions from a New Testament Perspective*

- *Woodpecker Wars: Celebrating the Spirituality of Everyday Life*

- *95 Tweets: Celebrating Martin Luther in the 21st Century*

- *How Big is Your Tent? A Call for Christian Unity, Tolerance, and Love*

Be the first to hear about Peter's new books and receive updates at PeterDeHaan.com/updates.

Printed in Great Britain
by Amazon